The American Family

The

American Family

a history in photographs

Jeffrey Simpson

A Studio Book · The Viking Press · New York

Acknowledgements

The author of a book covering such a broad topic as the American family must be heavily indebted to other people's knowledge and art. Certain books have been particularly enlightening and useful to me: Mary Cable's *American Manners and Morals* (American Heritage, 1969); Robert and Helen M. Lynd's seminal and fascinating *Middletown* (Copyright 1929 by Harcourt Brace Jovanovich, Inc., © 1956 by Robert S. Lynd and Helen Merrill Lynd); Daniel Boorstin's *The Americans: The National Experience* and *The Americans: The Democratic Experience* (Random House, 1965, 1974). Excerpts and ideas from these and other books and articles—including Lisa Alther's *Kinflicks* (Knopf, 1976); C. D. B. Bryan's *Friendly Fire* (Putnam's, 1976); Paul Engle's "An Iowa Christmas," *American Heritage*, December 1967; Joseph Epstein's *Divorced in America* (Dutton, © 1974 by Joseph Epstein); Robert Fitzgerald's "Notes on a Distant Prospect," *The New Yorker*, February 23, 1976; Hannah Green's *The Dead of the House* (Doubleday, 1972); Alexis de Tocqueville's *Democracy in America* (Harper and Row, © 1966 in the English translation by Harper and Row); Eudora Welty's *Losing Battles* (Random House, ©1970 by Eudora Welty); and Laura Ingalls Wilder's *The Long Winter* and *These Happy Golden Years* (Harper and Row, 1952)—will be found in these pages. All are reprinted by permission, and enrich the text immensely.

Both the photographers, whose interpretive art provides the manifold views of Americans in this book, and the curators and staff of the museums and agencies where these photographs are kept have been extremely helpful. I would especially like to thank Gerard Reese and Amelia Bielaski of the New York State Historical Association, Cooperstown, New York; Jerry Kearns of the Library of Congress; Robert Jackson and Tom Logan of Culver Pictures; Joan Lifton and Geoffrey Biddle of Magnum Photos; Martha Jenks of George Eastman House; and the research staff of The Bettmann Archive for their patience as well as their help.

Certain people have been consistently generous with their advice and expertise. Margaretta Barton Colt applied her professional picture editor's knowledge to the book in its early stages and was very helpful in selecting a core of material to build on. Penelope Morgan Colman performed the essential function of helping to structure the book at a critical point in its development. Daniel Jones provided material from his extensive collection of American photography, as well as his time and expertise. Marcia Bell was kindly supportive and applied critical judgment to the book at all stages.

The staff of Studio Books at The Viking Press were unceasing in their professional attention as well as being entirely gracious to the author, who was ever present in the Studio offices during the past six months. Jacqueline Bouvier Onassis brought a fresh eye and judgment to a mass of photographs at an inchoate stage of the book. Olga Zaferatos' high critical standards for the manuscript have been invaluable. Christopher Holme's imaginative design brought out the content of each photograph to its full richness. Gael Dillon was thoroughly professional in her design assistance. Ellyn Childs Allison's meticulously intelligent editing of the text was the best kind of collaboration there could be.

I am especially grateful to all the friends, colleagues, and families who expressed interest in the book and who permitted me to look at the treasures in their own family albums.

Finally, I am indebted to all the photographers who have captured the American family in all its variety and points of similarity since the time of the first daguerreotype.

Library of Congress Cataloging in Publication Data

Simpson, Jeffrey.
   The American family: a history in photographs.
   (A Studio book)
   1. Family—United States—History. I. Title.
HQ535.S48   301.41X2X0973   76-25069
ISBN 0-670-11817-6

Contents

For my parents,
whose love gave me the best sense of family,
and
for my editor, David Bell,
without whose prompting and participation
this book could not have come to be.

Introduction

During the ten years between 1840 and 1850, when the first daguerreotype studio multiplied itself a thousandfold, recording the family image became possible for just about everyone. People assembled albums full of *carte-de-visite* photographs—small rectangles of pasteboard with a positive image of an individual or couple glued onto them. The term *carte-de-visite* implied that these squares would replace the ordinary visiting card which just had the bearer's name printed on it; in fact, few people used them this way, but the idea was curiously apt: Long before the day of the I.D. card with a laminated image of the bearer, the photograph established a person's identity with a wholly new certainty and, indeed, inescapability. Before 1850 there had been little to prevent a man from walking to a town twenty-five miles from home, giving a fictitious name as his own, and assuming a whole new persona with little fear of detection.

As photographs gave individuals an image of themselves that they had to live up to and could not escape from, so pictures of a family clarified the family image. The middle classes could assume what had been a privilege of the rich and trace family resemblances and characteristics back for a generation or two at least. Family albums—those thick books bound in velvet with covers of ivorylike celluloid and stiff pages of stiff portraits—were placed in every American home on the parlor table next to the family Bible. The latter recorded births and deaths and marriages, the former recorded the faces. Together, they made a shrine of domestic piety, the influence of which no family member could hope to permanently escape. If a scapegrace uncle disappeared in the West, there was his photograph to remind future generations of his transgressions.

When George Eastman sold the first "Kodak" in 1888, the possibilities for recording people's life at home in every snapshot were manifold. Recording daily experience made traditions out of small family events. If the album contained a snapshot of a baby girl sitting under the rose arbor in the backyard taken in 1910, the odds were that when the girl grew up, she would want to photograph her own baby in the same spot in 1935; the Christmas dinner table, for instance, could be reconstructed precisely from the snapshot of the year before. What had been merely domestic habits were formalized by the photographic record into rituals. Life imitated the photographic image in all sorts of ways. In *American Manners and Morals*, historian Mary Cable remarks that before the 1940s wedding photographs were posed and stiff, but after the appearance of *Life* and the other great magazines of photojournalism every photographer had to take a series of candid shots for the bride's album. The style of magazine photography had influenced private life. The wedding was of course somewhat structured by the participants' knowledge that their tears and smiles and best lace handkerchiefs would all be preserved forever on film. The photographers who worked for the big picture magazines and the contemporary camera fiends who pour out of every college class have all made the family the subject of professional observation, but the effect of photographs that immortalize lives as they are lived is basically the same, whether they are done by professionals or by Mother who snaps a scene with her Brownie. The recorded image preserves the past and provides a model for the future.

Just as certain faces stand out in a collection of family photographs, so certain facts about our whole national identity become clear when one considers the American family as it was and is. This is in large part because the family has traditionally been our strongest social unit. The decision to join one's life to another person's has always had particular social force in America. In the great wilderness that covered much of the continent for the first 250 years of settlement, the only community that Pa, Ma, and the children knew was their own family group. Towns, when they existed, exercised little control over self-sufficient farms; state government was trackless miles away; Washington was a muddy site by the Potomac where a national government presided that was as aspiring and fragmentary as the jagged splinter of Washington Monument, which stood half finished during most of the nineteenth century. Those independent American families who exercised complete control over their own homesteads began with the union of two free and independent Americans, and the first photograph in this book is, appropriately, that of a couple. Couples are, rather obviously, the basic unit of the family. No matter what happens afterward, there would have been no family if two people had not come together, decided to make a life and probably rear children together. The pair in the frontispiece were photographed in 1850. They have left no names or occupations for us, but some inferences can be drawn from the photograph: They were probably Easterners because the man's elaborate cravat and satin vest were in the height of fashion then, and a Westerner could not have obtained them with any ease; they may have been well-to-do, but we cannot be sure, because the formality of the time demanded a certain standard of dress from all middle-class, independent citizens, and every American considered himself just that. One other fact that we can bring to bear, here, is the average age of marriage in 1850: twenty-two for men and twenty for women. Those are older than the average ages today, and our couple were probably old enough to be undertaking a considered responsibility.

This couple who decided to build a new life together may stand as a metaphor for America itself, for their circumstances mirror the experience of the nation as a whole. Just as they seem independent and most likely chose each other without parental interference (from the 1700s on European travelers remarked with amazement that American girls chose husbands "according to their fancy"); so, with similar independence and freedom, most immigrants to the New World (with the exception of blacks) chose to build a new life and new community together. Just as our couple show by their clothes that they felt the importance of prosperity, so most Americans, in the words of Alexis de Tocqueville, have "set immense value on their possessions" and felt themselves entitled to the best. Just as this couple's background cannot be deduced from their appearance, so most immigrants shed their original cultures and became more American than Irish or German or Italian within a generation or two. And just as this couple would produce a unique family from their union, so the many peoples settling the continent would together breed a new and distinct race. The American experience of birth and growth for more than two hundred years was comparable on an immense scale to what happened in every individual family. Between the late seventeenth century and the early twentieth, when the first quotas on immigration were set, a new race with distinctive speech, social patterns, expectation, and, to some degree, appearance was generated almost as fast as new families were created.

Now that America is living through its middle age, a period of consumption rather than expansion, the precise value of the family is being questioned because the traditional family experience of marriage, birth, and building a new life is out of step with the national experience. We have built our country, we have settled our frontiers, we have mined the land, we have dammed the rivers and, yet, at home we are subject to the primitive government of the family and must cultivate and nurture and build our private lives from scratch in the old way. Furthermore, because national experience did parallel the family's for so much of our history, the needs of the state and the needs of the family became identified; now that national needs are complex and changing, the family is required to attempt to change also.

The change will more likely lie within the family structure than eliminate it altogether. People need more than fleeting encounters with strangers and a guardian state in order to satisfy the desire for intimacy and companionship. The social units that are expected by some to replace the family—the communes surviving from the 1960s, the couples who choose to live together but not marry—come to resemble families if they endure for any length of time at all. The care of children will remain a social necessity, and the family will remain the most efficient and immediate agent for handling it, although new career opportunities for women and their greater involvement in the world outside the home will alter responsibilities within the family. One of the strongest reasons for the survival of the family is economic. In 1976 half of the families in the United States had an annual income under $12,500; ninety percent had less than $22,000. When there are two or more children in a family, these incomes will not stretch to pay for the services of agencies outside the home that might take over family duties, nor can people pay enough in taxes to permit the government to efficiently assume them. People cannot afford to give up the family, and as long as men and women want some contact and context beyond what their senses provide—as long as the sound of their own blood humming through the veins is not enough to break the lonely stillness of the night—they will not want to give up the family.

To forecast the future of the American family is beyond the scope of this book, but from the close examination of the present that the camera affords, inferences about the future can be drawn. These portfolios of photographs and textual introductions are intended to describe what the American family experience has been since the first relatively spontaneous images of it were recorded by the camera. The essays that introduce each portfolio are intended to serve as illustrations would in an ordinary book—to sharpen impressions and place information in perspective; the photographs should be regarded as "text," for they tell the story. The pictures show the American family as a microcosm of the American nation and reveal the many points at which the national experience touches the lives of families.

The widowed prairie father who cared for his children in a sod hut (page 143) was one of the thousands enduring hardship in the hope of future plenty; the anxiety of the Depression-ridden country in 1936 furrowed the brow of the very young Ohio father (page 146) who wondered how he could shelter and feed his wife and child; the adolescents who smoked daringly in the 1920s (page 181) and bought identical straw "skimmers" in the 1930s (page 180) and teased their hair in the 1950s (page 181) reflected the increasing power of the peer groups that radio and movies and television were bringing together in common experience; the grandmothers of the 1950s and 1960s who lectured and played with their grandchildren (pages 198–201) were trying to adjust to a world of nuclear families with houses too small for three generations.

The last photograph in the book shows a couple, as does the first. But while the first couple are young and stern and expectant, the last is old and laughing and content. They have a full table of Thanksgiving turkey before them, they know each other's ways completely, and they are fond. If the American family in its middle age is reflected in the virtues and good fortune of this couple, we are happy.

Before 1876

Before 1837, when the first camera recorded a corner of a French inventor's studio, nobody really knew what families other than their own and those of some neighbors looked like. Only the rich could have their portraits painted—a lengthy and expensive process—and it was usually impractical and too costly even for the rich to commission portraits of whole family groups. To be sure, resplendent paintings have been made since medieval times of European royal families, all swathed in brocade and buttressed with marble columns—the faces of the eight, or ten, or sixteen little princes and princesses looking as though they had been painted separately and stuck onto the group portrait after the columns and the cloth were done. There were also "conversation pieces," voguish among the eighteenth-century English aristocracy, which were meant to depict conversation rather than provoke it; consequently, they show large groups of noble Englishmen and Englishwomen engaged in such informal pastimes as preparing for a hunt or playing cards. But these family group portraits were rare and scarcely existed at all in America. One variation of the English conversation piece ordered by some prosperous New Englanders was what we would call a "primitive." These paintings were done by an itinerant "limner," who appeared in a village with his canvases all painted, except for the faces. The individual figures stood stiffly against flat backgrounds, or a woman's figure sat on one side of a table, a man's on the other, and several sexless little figures in the white dresses that boys and girls used to wear stood in front. The limner would then paint in the faces of the family that bought the picture—not the most spontaneous family representation.

And then came photography: photography that made available the preserved "memory" of the rich to everyone. Within fifteen years of Samuel Finley Breese Morse's return in 1839 from a trip to Europe with the first camera America had ever seen, every American country village had a "daguerreotypist" with a studio where any family could come to be immortalized on copper. *The New York Tribune* calculated that New York City photographers took three million pictures in 1855. At first the mechanical portraits were not so very different from the best painted ones in the old days. Exposure time ranged from a minute up, and the sitters had to remain perfectly motionless, often with their heads in a viselike clamp. The result was a crystal-clear rendering—of an unnatural situation and pose.

The function filled by early family photographs was the same as the function of a painted portrait. A daguerreotype was thought of as a once- (or twice-) in-a-lifetime record, not only of faces, but of the prosperity and coherence of a family. It was meant to record that a family had leisure, clothes, and money enough—and sufficient sense of itself and as an acceptable social unit—to get together, get dressed up, and defy time, to become part of posterity. In turn, the photograph itself became testimony of these qualities it was meant to denote. "They were people of enough consequence to have their likenesses taken" would come to mean "They must have been people of consequence because they had their likenesses taken"—at least in the minds of the sitters' descendants.

What were they like—those American families who harnessed themselves into corsets and high collars; boiled the children's clothes in water drawn from the well and set over a fire of hand-hewn wood; fed and hitched up a horse and then rode over bumpy dirt tracks for several hours, perhaps, to the studio of the daguerreotype "professor"? In the first place, they probably lived on a farm. In the census of 1870, it was recorded that more than half the population of the United States (six out of every eleven workers) made their living by agriculture. This meant that it was advantageous to have as many people in the family as possible to supply workers for the farm. But the twentieth-century assumption that before 1900 all American families were made up of several generations, living together in a comfortable rambling house, is prompted more

(1) *The great and terrible Civil War divided the nation and split families asunder. General Edward Ord of the Grand Army of the Republic is shown on all-too-brief leave in Washington in this photograph by the famous Mathew Brady. The sadness of Ord and his family gives the portrait an intimacy rare in the days of stiff poses and long camera exposure times.*

11

by sentiment than by accuracy. We think of the nineteenth century as a prosperous landscape dotted with big houses, like a Currier & Ives engraving, because, as sociologist William J. Goode has pointed out, the big houses were the ones that were well built and so they are the ones that survive. Cabins were abandoned or incorporated into larger houses, but there were plenty of them, and the families were not so big as our collective memory indicates. According to the first United States census, of 1790, the average number of persons in a household was six; in 1965 the average was four. It is true, in distinction to most of our households, those six might include a grandparent or unmarried aunt or uncle because different generations often stayed together to help coax a living from the land they lived on.

Such a farm family in the 1850s or 1860s probably was descended from pre-Revolutionary Anglo-Saxon forebears, or else they were recent immigrants from Northern Europe—Germany or Scandinavia. The Irish who began to emigrate in great numbers after the Potato Famine of 1849 became an urban people who rose to middle-class estate in the mills and political wards of the towns.

In the third quarter of the nineteenth century, many Americans lived close to or in the house where they had been born. But moving on had always been an option in a country where a vast tract of plains and mountains west of the Mississippi proclaimed the nation's manifest destiny to expand. When the Homestead Act was passed in 1862, 160 acres of open government land became available to any citizen, either for a minimal purchase price or for merely living on for six years, if he were patient. Ever since the first pioneers had crossed the Allegheny Mountains in the eighteenth century, many a young man carried the dream of "going West" in his head, as he plowed his father's rocky Eastern fields and husked his father's corn. During the first three quarters of the nineteenth century, most communities saw several families move West, and many families lost at least one member to the new land. The chance of moving, getting out, made America, despite its concentration around the small town and the family farm, always aware of the power of the young. In classbound Europe, a young man's only chance to avoid repeating his father's life was to run away to America; natives here had only to go beyond the last outpost, and that fact gave young people a self-confidence and a power. Children were more important to parents—they were needed to help on the family farm—than parents were to children. In the West especially, there were as many young families composed of father, mother, and child (what we would call today "nuclear" families) as there were extended families of several generations. The potential independence from authority that young people enjoyed, together with the management of their own affairs, formed a base for democratic government. Many of them wrested land and sustenance from the wilderness, and they wanted to protect what they had gained single-handedly. They knew they were capable of self-government, and there was enough at stake to make self-government worth the effort.

Actually, not quite everyone had a voice in government or the chance of mobility. The 300,000 Indians living in their extended-family tribes in 1870 attempted to maintain a primeval—and usually nomadic—way of life against the white man's greed for land, against disease, and against organized persecution leveled by settlers and government agencies. The Indian population in the West declined along with the staples of their life—the buffalo and other wildlife. There were more than two hundred battles between Indians and whites between the close of the Civil War and 1875; the number of buffalo slaughtered was in the millions. Mobile as much by the necessity of flight as by choice, the Indian was totally without a voice in any government beyond his tribal councils.

In contrast to the Indians' mobility, the 4 million black people who lived in this country in 1860 were mostly slaves, bound to their owners. After 1865 those blacks, although legally free, for almost another century were held in economic servitude to white landowners, who furnished them life's bare necessities. Still, the fact of slavery had been the breaking point in the political power struggle between the Northern and Southern states and one of the primary causes for the devastating Civil War. It was the first, and to date the most violent, expression of the American concern for minorities.

For the black minority, family life differed sharply from white domesticity. Many slaveholders actively discouraged the extralegal marriages performed by slave preachers. Members of black families were liable to be sullen and not work well if sold separately, and white owners were more likely to have trouble asserting their rights de seigneur with a slave woman who considered herself someone else's wife. Consequently, many black women and their children were a family unto themselves.

This strongly matriarchal family was in sharp distinction to the white American families before 1870, in which "Papa" or "Pa" was usually accorded the position of the Victorian patriarch whose word was law and whose wife's total lack of legal rights bore out her husband's authority. Although the scarcity of women in colonial times had made them valuable and given them leverage in the choice of suitors and even given them property rights, by the mid-nineteenth century Victorian convention had reduced American women to dependency status—along with children, criminals, the insane, and blacks. All of a woman's property became her husband's when she married; until 1882 he even owned her clothes and jewelry, and he could lawfully beat her as long as he used "a reasonable instrument." The children who had to be conceived in large numbers to insure the survival of a very few were also, usually, the decision and "right" of a husband. Women going into marriage were supposed to be completely ignorant of sex; if they were prepared at all it was with the news that men had animal lusts that women must submit to with Christian forbearance. Women, needless to say, were not expected to enjoy anything involving Christian forbearance. But by the end of the 1860s, new economic opportunities for women—mostly menial work in the mills and shops—provided some alternative to complete dependence. In any case, as sociologist Robert Bales has pointed out, almost any unit of people working or living together (the American family before 1870 usually did both) has one leader who sets goals and provides motivation—someone who makes the "big decisions"—and another leader who implements the actual work and keeps things running smoothly among all members. The mother in a family, cast in the latter role, could alleviate her legal nonexistence with the considerable influence that belongs to someone who actually gets things done.

Getting things done, of course, involved much more physical labor in 1860 than it does today. The farmer's day started at 5:00 A.M., and practically every article of food or clothing, except the luxuries—tea, coffee, sugar, and salt—had to be grown or nurtured, and then harvested or shorn, canned or woven into its final form by the family themselves. In the cities, work was also seen as man's natural condition, and even well-to-do entrepreneurs worked more than ten hours a day with only the Sabbath on which to rest—in church. At home in the city it was back-breaking labor to take down twenty-pound portieres and take up thirty-pound carpets that could only be cleaned by beating or sweeping. Because everything took so much longer to accomplish than it does today, people were reconciled to a slower pace of work. We like to think there was not so much pressure. In fact, the pressure was of a less frequent but more severe order; a farmer might have slack months in the winter when he could sit near a red-hot stove and whittle and contemplate the frost patterns on the windowpane, but there might come that one night in the fall when an early frost would ruin a whole crop and destroy a family's food supply and income. The fact that children today are impelled by social pressures to differ radically from their parents can hardly cause a modern mother more anguish than that suffered by a nineteenth-century mother because of the death of three of four children.

Death, it has been said, assumes the taboo place in our world that sex had in the nineteenth century. We regard mentioning it to be in poor taste; and, with nursing homes multiplying, it seems that we regard even its intrusion in the form of sick friends or dying members of the family to be in poor taste, too. People in the nineteenth century could not ignore death by putting the sick in hospitals and the dead in funeral parlors. Death struck suddenly and often, and struck at home. The dead were washed and clothed for their last journey by those who had known them in life.

Thus the ten families that look out from these photographs stiffly, usually proudly, a little diffident before the "professor" and his dark cloth and strange machine embody the concerns that involved most American families before 1876. The Indian and black minorities found life almost unbearably harsh; they were an unresolved problem for the white majority so that the nation was rent by the Civil War and the frontier was shredded by constant skirmishing. Mobility was an alternative and a challenge for most white families; and for farming families something of a threat. Death was a more frequent and sudden intruder then than now, and the nineteenth-century American was fascinated by death (he was generally more theologically oriented than we tend to be). There were more extended families, with adult children or grandparents living at home, than is usual now. But perhaps the most important point about these pictures is that they make us feel not how different these people were from us, their descendants, but how similar. We know the groups in these photographs are families because they are pictured with children, and the implication is that they are raising them. They were proud enough of themselves to have their likenesses taken together, and they seem to have felt that they were at a high point in their lives worth recording. It is not too much to say that faith in the future—and the young who bring it—was a particularly American trust. These families are confident that, if they do their part, they will have their chance.

2

Ninety percent of the population of the United States lived in rural areas before the Civil War, but the way of life on the farms of the settled East was very different from that on the plains of the West. (2) In 1865 the Steeres were photographed outside their homestead near Cooperstown, New York. Several generations have gathered together for the Sunday afternoon visit that constituted the principal social event of the week for many big families.

(3) *For American Indians, who were as family and tribe oriented as the Steeres could ever have been, there was less and less territory to gather on as the nineteenth century waned. This Cheyenne family had survived many clashes between white soldiers and Indian tribes when they pitched this summer camp on the northern plains. They are drying meat for winter; on the right are entrails which will be stuffed into sausages like those hanging at the left.* (4) *Nomadic white families moving West tried to maintain Eastern amenities while they adjusted to frontier conditions. It might take six months to cross flooding rivers, mountains, and prairies. One diary mentioned "victuals crusted not with sugar but with snow."*

6

American families were often fragmented by death and poverty in the
nineteenth century, and the jolly woman with her three
children (5) may be a widow. She has kept the girls dressed in proper
style for the 1850s; but high-button shoes, drawers, petticoats, and the
broad-brimmed hat to preserve a ladylike complexion have not
dampened their high spirits. The woman's wedding ring is on her
right hand, a practice customary here in the nineteenth century, and
still customary in Europe. (6) Mrs. Van Patten of Middlefield Center,
in upstate New York, went to the daguerreotype "professor," new
bonnet on her head, husband and baby in tow, in 1858. The child is
probably a boy—both sexes wore dresses until six or seven years of
age. His velvet cap and Mr. Van Patten's satin vest indicate that the
family were probably not farmers, who would not have had ready
cash for luxuries. (7) "David Reeves, 1862," is the only notation on
this tintype of grandparents and grandson. Nineteenth-century
grandparents often brought up a family of grandchildren to help
them on their farm and relieve the burden of parents with many
offspring.

Life was harsh for all nineteenth-century Americans, but not equally so. (8) For black Americans there were no amenities. Relaxation meant dropping from exhaustion, and there was nothing but bare earth to fall on. Slave cabins never had wooden floors, and the earth between the cabins was pounded flat because grass and gardens were too much trouble to keep. Ironically, though several generations often slept in one room, blacks had little coherent family life because they could not be legally married, women could be forced into sexual relations with their masters, and family members could be sold separately. (9) White Southern slaveholders usually had a strong sense of family because they were tied to the family land and its one crop of cotton, tobacco, or rice. The Honorable John Minor Botts of Virginia was the embodiment of the Victorian patriarch in this photograph, with his wife standing respectfully to his right on the veranda. Mr. Botts was also one of the exceptional Southerners who opposed the secession of Virginia from the Union, and he spent some of the Civil War in a Southern prison writing a secret history of the conflict.

(10) *Death was a common fact of life in the early republic, and funerals were frequent social rituals. The family at this 1870s Indiana funeral has purchased a modern and elaborate coffin for the deceased—perhaps the reason for the photograph. Fifteen years earlier, the coffin would have been a wedge-shaped box of a type unchanged since the Middle Ages. The scene is grim, despite its refinements and its familiarity for the participants.*

The Public Image–
How the Family Sees Itself

The early daguerreotypes were formal family documents, and photography has continued to serve this function long beyond the time of the huge, immobile cameras and minute-long exposures. Modern studio portraits of a family or such a family occasion as a wedding share many of the characteristics of the first photographs. Studio portraiture tends to be static and posed and is meant to display a family's material position and unity. To some extent, a studio portrait is controlled by the photographer who poses the family, chooses a backdrop, and tells everyone to "watch the birdie" or say "cheese." But the decision to have a formal portrait taken is the family's alone. They want an image recorded, and it is a public image. It reflects how they hope they appear to their world.

In the third photograph in this section, a portrait of the Buckners, a black family who lived in Lawrence, Kansas, about 1912, aspiration to a dignified public image is rather touchingly evident. Mrs. Buckner wears a fashionable suit of the period, with the high lace collar and feathered hat that the most prominent matrons affected. The clothes look natural and suit her well; the only evidence of strain is her tired gaze off to the side of the picture. Mr. Buckner was a guard at the Merchants National Bank, according to the lettering on the band of his cap. He wears his uniform, which is more the way a social documentarian than a portraitist would photograph him, but, we may conjecture, he had no other formal clothes to wear, and he was perhaps proud of his responsible job and dressy cap. Then, there is the cap of the oldest child, who stands between her parents; this cap, maybe a hand-me-down or gift, was large so that the girl could grow into it. Her hair ribbons, necessary adornment for nice little girls of the time, are stuffed awkwardly under the hat. It is only Mrs. Buckner—and possibly the two babies in their immaculate knit suits—who has managed to achieve the fashionable middle-class look that a family portrait is supposed to convey.

Public-image family portraits always make at least one statement about what a family wants to be like, and often they make another about social conditions or personal feelings that the family is often only dimly aware of or wishes to hide. These secondary disclosures in a formal family portrait are not necessarily negative or hidden, however. The portrait of the Recknagel family of Round Top, Texas, taken around 1895 by Frederike Michaelis Recknagel, the woman in the photograph, has several unusual features. The composition and the surroundings are extraordinarily sophisticated; it is the woman who is sitting—not, as was more usual, the head of the house—and the subjects are grouped in at least a simulation of natural poses. The traditional family portrait shows everyone facing the camera, outlined against the backdrop like paper dolls that can be cut out and put to any use. Here the profession of Frederike Recknagel, a photographer of note in the Texas hill country, becomes part of the composition, for she has portrayed herself, her husband, and her child looking at her own photographs. There is an intention here of depicting warmth and strong ties that is generally not present in public-image photographs, which mostly show the wished-for relationship of the family to society. Frederike Recknagel and her family have carefully, formally constructed an image of the relationship among themselves for society to envy.

The least personal portraits, of course, are those that existed before photography, in which a royal family established the fact that a position of authority had been filled. The image of a king or president on a coin reassured people that the king or president really existed. Somebody was at the helm. For private individuals, time wreaks such changes that they may want to record the moments when they were happiest or

(11) *Frederike Michaelis Recknagel posed herself, her husband, Eduard, and her daughter, Louisa, looking at Frederike's own photographs in the 1890s. Mrs. Recknagel was a member of the community of cultivated Germans who emigrated to Texas in the 1840s. The traditional German interest in the arts might explain Frederike's elegant technique, which here produced what is virtually an icon of a perfect family, rather than merely a portrait.*

12

13

(12) *Willie Babbitt was a "cracker" who worked as caretaker of the Florida orange grove owned by a rich Northern family. About 1905 he gathered his motherless brood for the photographer. Crackers were the poorest whites in Georgia and Florida, who got their name from the whips they cracked driving skinny cattle through the piny woods. In the backwoods, it was women who upheld standards of gentility; Willie's daughters have put on shoes and hats for the camera, but Willie and his boys wear their work clothes.* (13) *The photographer's caption for this portrait of the Buckner family of Lawrence, Kansas, in 1912 was simply "Buckner and family." No matter how prosperous, a black man in pre–World War I America was rarely given the dignity of the title "Mr."* (14) *Evalyn Walsh McLean was an heiress and the Washington, D.C., society matron who owned the Hope diamond, furnished with its own Indian curse. Mrs. McLean posed with her son in Palm Beach in 1912. Mrs. McLean and Mrs. Buckner had the same notion of elegance, but the plumes in Mrs. McLean's hat are egret feathers, taken from birds whose threatened extinction produced one of the first acts of ecology legislation in Congress in 1917.*

14

15

16

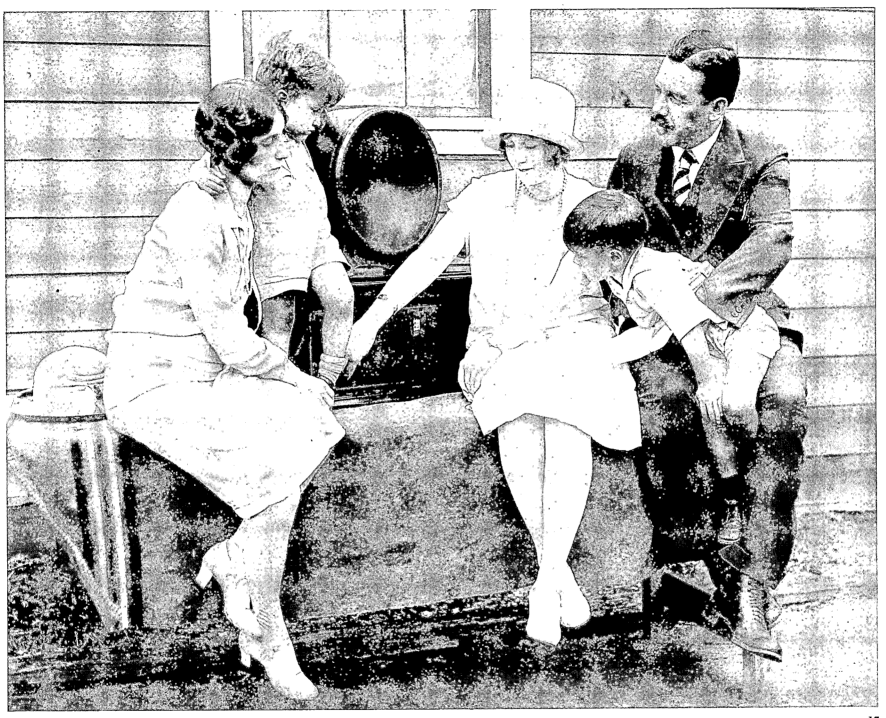

(15) *The Stewart sisters of Parnassus, Pennsylvania, had their photograph taken in 1905 when the oldest (far right) was twenty-eight and the youngest (far left) was sixteen. They were the daughters of a farmer and storekeeper who lived on land his ancestors settled in the late eighteenth century. (16) By 1920, when the Stewarts had their photograph taken again, two sisters had married businessmen, one a doctor, one a minister, one a newspaperman, and one a banker. No one remained on the family land, but the photograph attests to the sisters' image of themeselves as a united clan. (17) In 1928, Grover Whalen, official greeter for New York City, posed with friends—two mothers and their children—to show off a new Gramophone. Families—as upholders of the social order—made publicity photographs for the city legitimate and respectable.*

a

d

b

e

c

f

(18, 19) *The Talbert family of Redlands, California, have sent their family photograph as a Christmas card every year from 1946 to the present.*

Family Reunions

Now there was family everywhere, front gallery and back, tracking in and out of the company room, filling the bedrooms and kitchen, breasting the passage. The passageway itself was creaking; sometimes it swayed under the step and sometimes it seemed to tremble of itself, as the suspension bridge over the river at Banner had the reputation of doing. With chairs, beds, windowsills, steps, boxes, kegs, and buckets all taken up and little room left on the floor, they overflowed into the yard, and the men squatted down in the shade. Over in the pasture a baseball game had started up. The girls had the swing.

"Been coming too thick and fast for you?" Aunt Birdie asked Aunt Cleo.

"Everywheres I look is Beecham Beecham Beecham," she said.

EUDORA WELTY, *Losing Battles*

Americans have always been a mobile people. Before 1850, just about the time that photography became common, their mobility took the form of one or more sons' moving off alone into the brooding forest or the entire family's making the weary and difficult trek to some new land. In the first case, the children had only a very uncertain postal system to help them keep in touch with home; in the second, hometown roots were lost. Then, given those sensitive tentacles of the Industrial Revolution, the telegraph (1843) and the railroad (8,500 miles of track laid by 1850), communication opened up and people could get both to and from new land more easily. In addition, the industrialism that spawned the railroads made an alternative to home—the city—a more likely place to live. Many young people, in the burgeoning "brown decades" after the Civil War, when houses were painted liver-colored so that the soot from the ubiquitous belching mills wouldn't darken them so quickly, left the farm for the wages and chances of the big towns. For these new urban pioneers, there was no emotional relocation. It was hard to think of a frame house in a mill town as home. So, with new city wages and new railroad lines and new leisure, it was possible and attractive to go home. The ease with which this could be done was still only comparative, of course. It cost about ten dollars to go by rail from New York to Detroit in 1850, and a man's wages were likely to be only seven or eight dollars a week (the equivalent today would be a three-hundred-dollar ticket to London for a man earning 12,000 dollars a year); also, vacations in preunion days were rarely given, and paid vacations were unheard of. But it was possible to keep in touch by letter so that family members knew when the grandparents' golden wedding anniversary would be celebrated and, for a once-in-a-decade treat, it was possible to go home again. By the 1870s, the family reunion was a going concern.

Many small towns in the late nineteenth and early twentieth centuries formally organized reunions called Old Home Week, and everybody came back. On the whole subject of obsession with family reunions and the hometown, anthropologist Margaret Mead has remarked that until recently Americans, uprooted from their European past, were colonials in spirit and, furthermore, colonials from diverse backgrounds with no common past. Unlike two Englishmen in Africa who could reminisce about their common cultural hometown of London, a New Englander and a Southerner who met in Kansas would each have to rummage through his

Between 1905 and 1914, when the Carr-Todd family gatherings were held in Toddsville, New York (20, 21), reunions were highly organized affairs, with family historians, speeches, and tons of food. Toddsville had been founded by the grandfather of Samuel Todd (20, left front), one Jehiel Todd, who brought his family in oxcarts west from Connecticut in 1796. When the Todds and Carrs were photographed at the family graveyard (21), most of the early inhabitants of the town lay buried, and the cemetery wall pointed ominously at the assembled living Todds.

past in the hope of finding something in common with the other. Sharing a hometown, of course, was the best common experience. Mead says, "Each and every American has followed a long and winding road. . . . if the roads touched here, in this vast country where everyone is always moving, that is a miracle which brings men closer together." She remarks of American strangers meeting, "The same expectation underlies their first contact—that both of them have moved on and are moving on and that potential intimacy lies in paths that have crossed." Mead was writing in 1939 about an America much closer in behavior to that of 1900 than to ours today. In 1900 the importance of family paths that had been the same in the past was vivid to every uprooted person.

The occasion for these reunions that flourished then and that most of us have no familiarity with today was often the birthday of an aged patriarch or matriarch. The quotation that opens this chapter describes the gathering of a Mississippi hill-country clan in the 1930s for their granny's ninetieth birthday. Those people came from all over the state to the log farmhouse with its galleries and new tin roof (an improvement that keeps the out-of-town characters speculating about the hometown family's finances for most of the novel) to celebrate.

Sixty-five years or so before this fictional reunion, members of a family from Northfield, Vermont, came from much farther away to a reunion described in the *Northfield Watchman and Journal*, on July 12, 1871.

> Monday, the 10th, being the sixtieth birthday of our esteemed citizen, Hon. Heman Carpenter, of Northfield, it was appropriately observed by a family reunion at his home where he has lived for the last thirty-three years. All of the family now living were present, save one daughter-in-law and one grandson. Seated at the dinner-table were representatives of four generations. Principal among the many pleasant features of the day was the poem, read by Col. Geo. N. Carpenter, of Chicago, recounting the history of their early days, their old jokes, by-words, and familiar names, and the various matters of interest which had happened to the different members of the family—and the presentation of a beautiful and valuable gold-headed cane to his father, in behalf of all the children, by Jason H. Carpenter, of Milwaukee. A friend in the West had composed a very pretty instrumental piece of music, entitled "Memories of Home," which was dedicated to Mr. Carpenter, and was presented by his son-in-law, Dr. Edwin Porter, of Northfield. The Judge was not a little moved by these unexpected tributes of filial love and esteem, and in endeavoring to respond, was at first troubled to articulate but soon gained command of his feelings, and made a speech, fitting well the occasion. The day was one long to be remembered by those who participated in its enjoyments.

The first reunions to be characterized as such were usually rather formal, as we can tell from the *Watchman* article, and everyone dressed in his best bib and tucker. As time went on, the day-long celebration came to include a sporting element (Eudora Welty's men start up a baseball game). But there was always a recognition of why the group was all together: In *Losing Battles*, the hostess says this about past reunions, "Grandpa Vaughn . . . got the blessing said and the history [of the family] every bit delivered and the lesson of it through our heads before he even looked at the table." And there had to be food. Sometimes the two were combined. Sarah Orne Jewett's account of an 1890s Maine reunion includes a description of some remarkable desserts. "There was . . . elaborate reading matter on an excellent early-apple pie which we began to share and eat, precept upon precept. Mrs. Todd helped me generously to the whole word *Bowden*, and consumed *Reunion* herself . . . but the most renowned essay in cookery on the tables was a model of the old Bowden house made of durable gingerbread, with all the windows and doors in the right places." The quantity of food, of course, directly reflected the substance of the family, and it had to be prodigious. At the family reunion in *The Farm*, "there were three barbecued oxen and five lambs, as well as countless chickens, roasted with sweet corn and potatoes in the ashes of a fire which consumed several whole trees. There were cider and beer and cold water from the spring-house, and scores of pies. Sapphira's daughters and granddaughters and great-granddaughters served their relatives."

The recurring pattern of the reunions made them rituals as well as gatherings. There was always likely to be some "history" of the family either read as a homemade ballad or just recited in an oral tradition as old as Homer. Around 1900, when America was feeling flush after victory in the Spanish-American War, some big reunions assumed an increasingly genealogical aspect. This was the period when the Daughters of the

American Revolution, the Society of Mayflower Descendants, and many other organizations formed, virtually creating ancestors and a past for the young country, and the family reunions had their place in that movement. Some member of the extended family—extended to several hundred members—would have taken on the mantle of chronicler and genealogist. These genealogists would sometimes try to establish a connection with lofty, aristocratic European families (the "Hankeys of Fenway Park, Sussex, England" for a Pennsylvania-German family whose name was plainly the humble German name Henke).

The big reunions had business meetings and treasurers and all the apparatus of a club. They filled in the past for people whose future had diminished a little since the frontier had been pushed clear across the continent, and they made a community for people who presently lacked a stable one. But mostly the reunions were just plain fun. You could see everybody you ever knew, and gossip and eat and lie in the summer grass to your heart's content.

The big, clublike reunions seldom continued for more than fifteen or twenty years; by the 1920s the radio and the movies had by and large replaced them as entertainments. The smaller reunions—of twenty or so descendants of a particular couple—that were bonded with genuine family feeling still continue today in rural areas.

One form of the family reunion that continues, disguised in another ritual, is the funeral, as sociologist Robert Wernick suggests. "In fact, funeral attendance is perhaps a final tribute to the strength of family ties. It may be only a slight exaggeration to say that in many cases almost the only genuine family reunions these days take place in graveyards: Distant cousins with whom the dead person quarreled, and broke, ages ago, and in-laws who never bothered to turn up for Christmas dinner or a wedding celebration will come from miles away to see a member of the family return to Mother Earth." This is, indeed, a slight exaggeration, but many urban families, composed of father, mother, and one or two children, with parents who themselves came from small, rootless families will never know anything like the return to the land as a source of life that the best reunions provided for many an individual, long before his funeral.

The touch of the eternal that the family—the oldest group, community, and club known to man—and their reunions invoked was felt by Sarah Orne Jewett at the 1890s Bowden reunion. The family made a procession to tables set up in a grove. They walked four abreast and,

> as we moved along, the birds flew up out of the thick second crop of clover, and the bees hummed as if it still were June. There was a flashing of white gulls over the water where the fleet of boats rode the low waves together in the cove, swaying their small masts as if they kept time to our steps. The plash of the water could be heard faintly, yet still be heard; we might have been a company of ancient Greeks going to celebrate a victory, or to worship the god of harvests in the grove above. It was strangely moving to see this and to make part of it. The sky, the sea, have watched poor humanity at its rites so long; we were no more a New England family celebrating its own existence and simple progress; we carried the tokens and inheritance of all such households from which this had descended, and were only the latest of our line.

Family history was the excuse for a reunion; dinner was the real reason for it. Reunions were held in high summer so that the people who came could be accommodated outdoors and so that there would be fresh vegetables for the table. The "garden truck" complimented the hams, chickens, pies, cakes, pickles, and preserves that each woman brought in an attempt to outdo her relatives. Each age group was placed together (22) and there were gossip for the old folks and games for the young. Small cousins played "Run Sheep Run" and "Fox and Geese" and endured dares from bigger cousins who egged them into jumping out of the hayloft or going into the pen where the cantankerous old hog lived. (23) By 1940, when this reunion took place in Lawrenceburg, Kentucky, the automobile had made family visits more frequent and less of a special occasion. But after the big noon meal the men still moved outside and pitched horseshoes or just plain lazed around. The two girls in this photograph have moved as close to the men as they dared; if they had gotten closer, someone would have told them to get back to the porch.

24

(24–27) *The Jarrett family of Bakersville, North Carolina, have met on the second Sunday of August every year since 1928. Jane and John Jarrett had thirteen children, and ten of them were still living in 1966, when these photographs were taken. When the Jarretts drive out into the Appalachian mountain country to their reunion at the "home place," they do all the traditional things: New babies are cooed over by the older generations; fresh garden tomatoes, and baked beans and ham, scalloped potatoes, cole slaw, and candied sweet potatoes with marshmallows on top are served in the yard, and the young people politely wait for the older folks to go through the line first; and there's a visit to the cemetery to tend the family graves. At the Carr-Todds' reunion sixty years earlier (20, 21), a whole family community reassembled; the reunited Jarretts are just one extended family, and when the oldest generation of siblings dies out, the reunions probably will, too.*

25 26

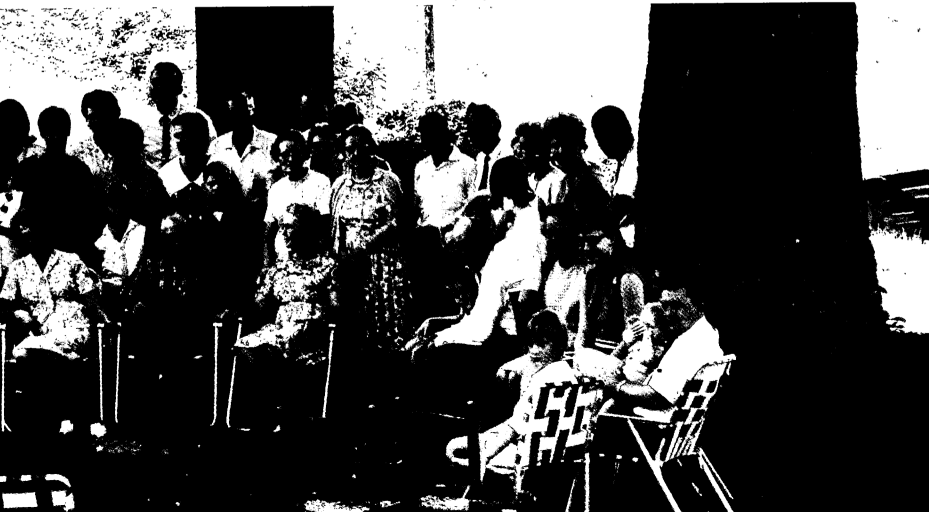

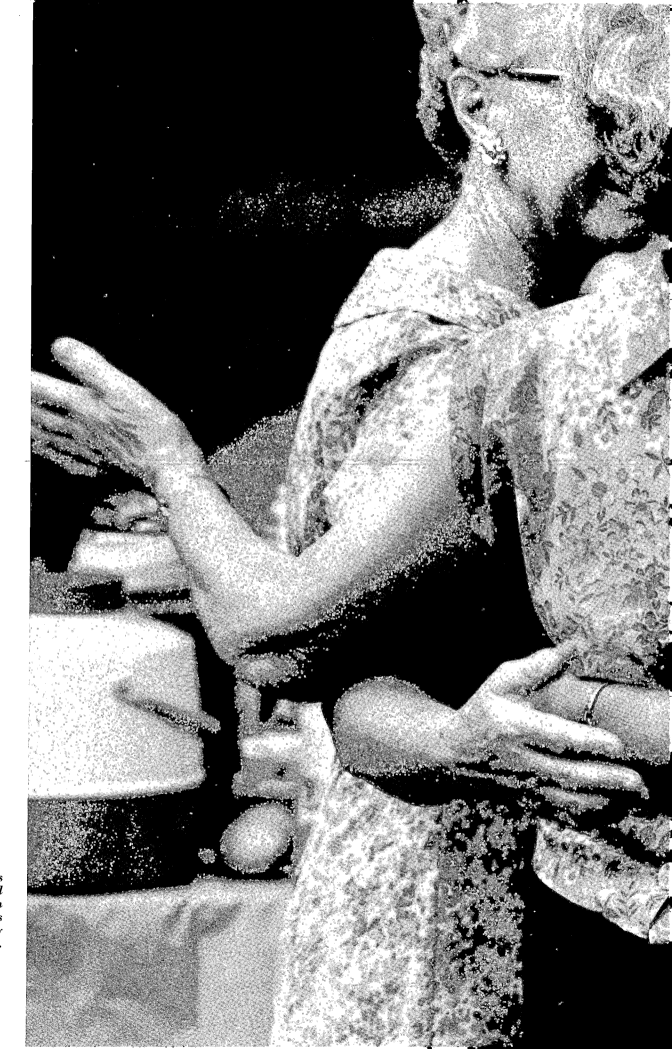

(28) *These three aging graces symbolize the impulse behind all reunions—recognition of the link with your own flesh and blood that years and distance never entirely extinguish.*

(29) *A Victorian patriarch could dominate his family even from beyond the grave, as
this portrait of the 1880s by the Boston photographer Charles Currier indicates.*

The Past As Family

> They talked about the past, really—always about the past. Even the future seemed like something gone and done with when they spoke of it. It did not seem an extension of their past, but a repetition of it.
>
> KATHERINE ANNE PORTER, *The Old Order*

Some kinds of family arrangements are more prevalent at certain periods of history than others. For centuries families sent their children to be "boarded out" or apprenticed with neighbors to learn a trade or a way of life different from what was found at home; in the early seventeenth century in New England and in the nineteenth century in the West, women were scarce, and every woman married and married young; in the latter half of the twentieth century, when children are an economic burden and careers for women offer an attractive alternative to domestic life, many couples who marry do not plan to have children. Any one of these customs was practical in its time but out of its time seems as bizarre as the harem of an Arab oil sheik. From the late seventeenth century to the mid-twentieth century, it was common in settled areas of the United States for adult unmarried children to continue living with their parents or with other adult siblings in the parental home. Now that custom, too, is passing by the board, as the young enjoy new sexual freedom and a wealth of job opportunities, and we look on those Victorian households composed of Mama and two or three unmarried daughters and say: "How stifling! How crushing that those children never fulfilled their potential."

But that, of course, is the point. Life had less career potential to offer young people in the nineteenth and early twentieth centuries, and there was also much less emphasis on the pursuit of personal potential. Instead of finding their identities and fulfilling themselves, docile parishioners were enjoined Sabbath after Sabbath from New England pulpits, the log podiums at camp-meetings, and gilded Catholic altars in immigrants' churches to do their duty. For those who listened, one duty was clear: the fifth commandment, "Honor thy father and thy mother," which included doing the tasks that their parents set before them. Young men might decide to slip out from under the parental yoke and go West to claim their own land or, later in the nineteenth century, venture off to the mills of the cities to seek their fortunes, but if you didn't choose this rather drastic course of leaving town like a criminal, there was no place like home respectably to lay your head and eat your supper. An unmarried woman could decently teach school but that almost certainly need not have taken her away from home. And, for offspring of either sex to insist on moving out of the house implied what the Victorians would call an "unwholesome" interest in privacy. It was generally felt that there should be no corner of a child's life that could not be exposed to the full glare of the family lamp in the middle of the parlor table. Reciprocally, the family protected the innocence of its children—especially its girls—from the snares of the outside world.

The effect of celibacy on family members who stayed at home is not too difficult to infer. Joseph Epstein, in his book *Divorced in America*, remarks, "People who have married . . . seem somehow to have lived more fully, to have experienced life at a deeper level than those who have never chanced the risky adventure of marriage in the first place. It is for this reason . . . that a lifelong bachelor, however worldly he may otherwise seem, in some regards remains callow." Epstein admittedly is writing as a man of the 1970s, but ever since the demise of the extended family living together, most profound human relationships may be said to occur between spouses and between parents and children. If one is deprived of the intensity of an adult relationship "at a deeper level" with a spouse, then one's most significant family bonds will be one's remembered relationship with one's parents *in the past.* Emotionally speaking, adult children with no marital bonds tended to live in the past. Often they never grew up. Sarah Orne Jewett, in a short story about Maine of the 1890s, described "such a household . . . where the parents linger until their children are far past middle age, and always keep them in a too childish and unworthy state of subjugation. The Misses Dobin's characters were much influenced by such an unnatural prolongation of the filial relationship, and they were amazingly slow to suspect that they were not so young as they used to be." The author goes on to say, "it was [their] nature to be girlish."

For the Victorians, the home was a fit object of *pietas*, even when no rich or famous ancestors had consecrated it by their presence. The attitude was intensified in America partly because the home has been one of the few stable cultural institutions in a mobile society. It was perhaps inevitable, then, that in the nineteenth century keeping up the house and all its little customs required the services of a domestic shrine-tender, often the maiden aunt. In *The House of the Seven Gables*, Miss Hepzibah Pyncheon "took a dreary and proud satisfaction in leading Phoebe from room to room of the house, and recounting the traditions with which . . . the walls were lugubriously frescoed." The domestic routine was exalted into ritual by people with no focus for their emotions beyond that routine itself. In the photograph on page 48 we see Abiantha Watkins and his daughter Carrie posed in Cooperstown, New York, in the 1890s; "Biathy" sits ruddy and complacent on the lawn while Carrie stands diffidently behind him. Her life would have been a round of maintaining Papa's routine and satisfying the whims that became as rigid as his joints and as arbitrary as if they came from royalty. The old gentleman is benignly selfish and confident that his well-fed, well-brushed comfort takes precedence over any claim of his daughter's to her own life. She has been kept so busily humble she can hardly lift her head to the camera lens. After all, every man's home was his castle, and maiden daughters were supposed to find the same degree of spiritual satisfaction from serving the lord of the house that a prime minister might from worthwhile service to the state.

Each detail of housekeeping in such a family was immutable. In her stories of small Iowa towns of the 1930s, Ruth Suckow describes one such old maid, who "not only loved her home but found her whole piety in that attachment. She was like a little aged Japanese woman intensely absorbed in a kind of ancestor, family, and finally place worship. But all drew down to earth, to objects, things—the house, the furniture, and that only because it had been used so long; the yard, the grass, the soil; the memory of those gone—the fixed sacredness of their ways."

Sometimes a trivial ritual, a hallowed piece of family etiquette, is reinforced by "the memory of those gone—the fixed sacredness of their ways." One unforgettable depiction of both the inflation of the trivial and the power of the past and its precedents was drawn by Elizabeth Gaskell, the nineteenth-century English writer, in her novel *Cranford*, which is about two old maids, Miss Deborah and Miss Matty Jenkyns.

> When oranges came in, a curious proceeding was gone through. Miss Jenkyns did not like to cut the fruit; for, as she observed, the juice all ran out nobody knew where; sucking (only I think she used some more recondite word) was in fact the only way of enjoying oranges; but then there was the unpleasant association with a ceremony gone through by little babies; and so, after dessert, in orange season, Miss Jenkyns and Miss Matty used to rise up, possess themselves each of an orange in silence, and withdraw to the privacy of their own room to indulge in sucking oranges.
>
> I had once or twice tried, on such occasions, to prevail on Miss Matty to stay, and had succeeded in her sister's lifetime. I held up a screen and did not look, and, as she said, she tried not to make the noise very offensive; but now that she was left alone [Miss Deborah Jenkyns has died], she seemed quite horrified when I begged her to remain with me in the warm dining-parlor, and enjoy her orange as she liked best. And so it was in everything. Miss Jenkyn's rules were made more stringent than ever, because the framer of them was gone where there could be no appeal.

It was the older Miss Jenkyns who dictated—even from beyond the grave—to the younger, and often it was this way in the old households of siblings, with assumption and delegation of authority having some of the dynamics of marriage. The household chores would be divided precisely, one sister perhaps doing the cooking and the other general housekeeping. The province of each was strictly respected, and often the one who did not cook was as helpless in the kitchen as any working man would be who depended on his wife to make meals. The stories in small towns of sisters living together for fifty years without speaking, or, conversely, becoming so habituated to the roles of leader and follower that, like Miss Matty Jenkyns, the one sister would not so much as eat an orange in the parlor unless directed by the other, parallel tales about Victorian marriages and the tensions and bonds that drained emotional energy in those airless alliances. But the difference between the relationship of elderly children at home and a marriage was that the siblings lived

36

37

Change within a pattern of continuity is fascinating to observe; when a life changes very little in outward form, the continuity between youth and age can be quite clear. The author's aunts, Nina and Marguerite Simpson of Parnassus, Pennsylvania, were left alone in 1912 to rear two younger brothers. (36) More than fifty years later (37), the brothers had long since married, but the sisters still lived together, and Marguerite's tilted head still seemed to question a future that had, in fact, become the past. (38) The author, the small boy in this portrait, was photographed with his family in Parnassus in 1951; he is the last member of three branches of his family. (39) The Hopi Indian cemetery at Acoma is rarely photographed because it is regarded as sacred, but it is often visited by grandmothers who want to impart a sense of the past of family and tribe to their grandchildren.

38

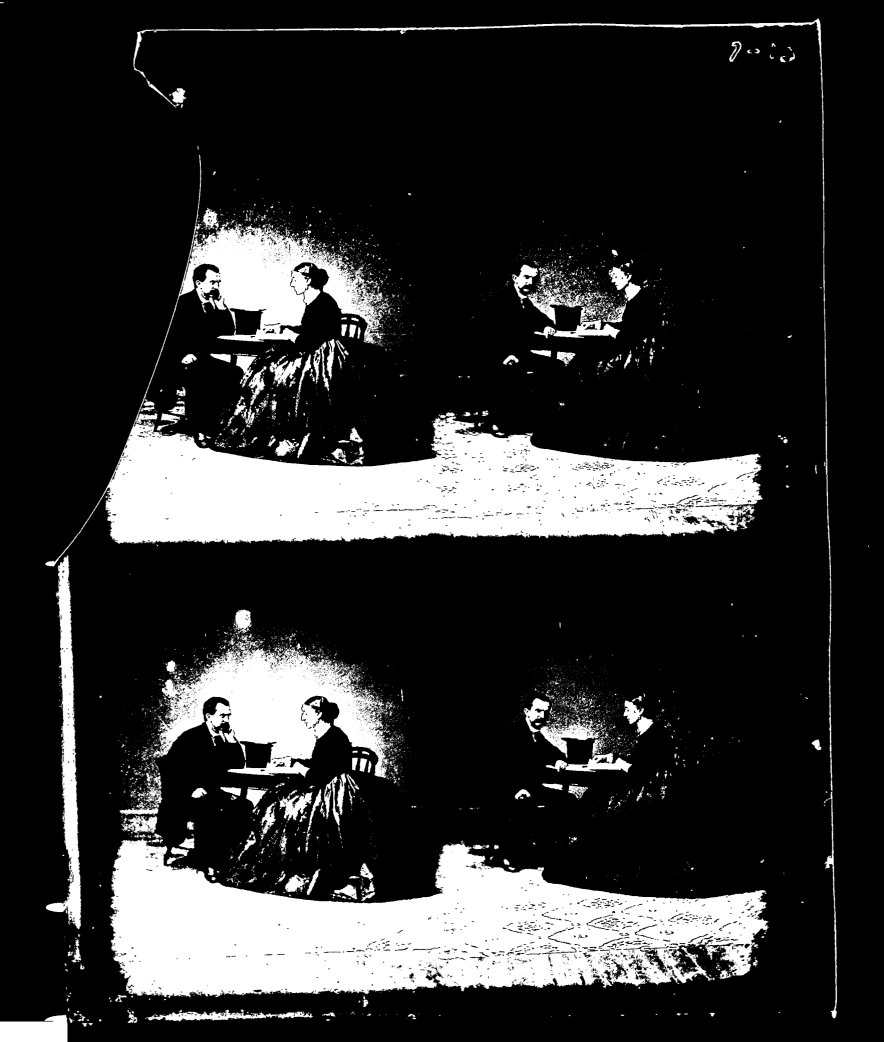

Courting

·Ever since Eve first offered Adam that apple—the legendary first courting in the world—and Captain Miles Standish sent John Alden to speak to Priscilla Mullins for him—the legendary first courting in America—men and women have been searching each other out with more or less serious intentions. Marriages may be made for economic reasons, for propagation, or simply to legalize the satisfaction of the sex urge because, as Saint Paul said, "It is better to marry than to burn [in hell]," but whatever the reason, there have to be preliminaries in which one person, usually the man, declares himself to the other.

In the early days of America, women were a much-prized minority and marriage a necessity to ensure the survival of the colonies and to make some kind of home life for their inhabitants. In 1642 women comprised only 10 percent of the population, and there was virtually no such thing as an unmarried female. Any woman who held out against marriage into her mid-twenties was thought to be antisocial and probably immoral; widows remarried within weeks of their husbands' deaths, and both sexes were likely to find several successive partners if they lived more than thirty or thirty-five years. These rigorous conditions made courtship a brief rite.

New Englanders particularly encouraged early marriages because the Puritan conscience held marriage to be a means of avoiding "unnatural pollutions, and other filthy practices in secret: and . . . horrid Murthers of the fruit of their bodies" (when premarital sex resulted in pregnancy). The Puritans, more realistic than our modern idea of them leads us to think, recognized the need for sexual relations between men and women and even encouraged them. One seventeenth-century divine went so far as to point out that "Lot was to blame that looked not out seasonably for some fit matches for his two daughters, which had formerly minded marriage . . . for they seeing no man like to come to them in a conjugall way . . . then they plotted that incestuous course, whereby their Father was so highly dishonoured." But, there still had to be preliminaries.

One of the most notorious American courting habits, most likely to provoke snickering and accusations of hypocrisy from later generations, was the practical solution to crowded space and the conservation of precious candles and firewood called "bundling." When a young couple bundled, the man calling on the young woman was tucked into the best bed with her, both of them fully dressed and sometimes with a board partitioning the covers between them; they thus found comfort and privacy while they got to know one another. Even during its seventeenth- and eighteenth-century heyday, bundling was a source of wild controversy, with those in favor pointing out that there was no other way for a couple to be alone in a cabin crowded with grandparents and babies. Besides, what harm could be wreaked by people wearing laced breeches and several petticoats, strapped in their respective places by three quilts and a board? You had to become acquainted with a future wife some way, declared one of the apologists, in verse.

> Man don't pretend to trust a friend to choose him sheep and cows,
> Much less a wife which all his life he doth expect to house.

(40) *A gentleman—and every nineteenth-century American male considered himself to be one—often made his first courting gesture by paying a call on a lady. Keeping your top hat with you, as this man did in the 1860s, meant that the call would be decorously short; still, a mother or married sister stayed in the room to protect warm-blooded young people from what a contemporary etiquette book called "extremes that they would themselves condemn, in a cooler moment." The modern mind wonders how extreme you could be in a fifteen-minute call wearing all those clothes.*

One of those opposed to the practice replied,

    But you will say that I'm unfair, that some who bundle take more care,
    For some we may in truth suppose, bundle in bed with all their clothes,
    But bundler's clothes are no defense, unruly horses push the fence.

Prudery increased with the new republic and the nineteenth century, as well as with larger houses, and bundling went out of style. But the reasons for defending bundling in the doggerel above reverberated with significance for three hundred years in America. The apologist who said a man must choose his own wife would have been thought crazy in most parts of the seventeenth-century world.

Free will in choosing a mate was a uniquely American custom. For most of the history of civilization, both Eastern and Western, marriage was regarded as an economic and civil contract involving the perpetuation and transfer of property rights. Therefore, it seemed only practical that those who owned the property, in most cases parents, should make the contract. Arranged marriages with payment made by one party to the other—often a dowry that a girl would bring her husband, whose property would then support her—were the rule. Until medieval troubadours began to sing of the possibility of gallant attentions between a knight and a lady, there had been no name since ancient times for the feelings of romantic love. The thought that romantic love could determine a matter as serious as the choosing of a lifelong mate would have struck the average seventeenth-century male as being as ridiculous as choosing a mate according to astrological predictions would strike most of us. And yet Americans were probably freed from arranged marriages by the same economic and practical considerations that established them in the Old World. Here, available land was not finite, as far as anyone knew. A man didn't need to marry a girl for her father's farm when he could strike a little farther out into the woods and carve a bigger farm of his own. Every American, from the first, felt himself as good as any other American. He had to find his own girl; and his prospects, when he found her, made him nearly as desirable as the greatest heir in town.

Free will, admittedly, was not complete. Most women needed their parents' consent to marry, partly because the dowry system held good until the American Revolution, but there were so few women available that if a maiden could not have her first choice for a husband, she could refuse her father's choice and still be fairly confident of being married eventually. Often, with the fresh breath of the New World in her lungs, the young American female followed her desire against her parents' will, with society's condonation. The editors of a column in the *Royal American Magazine* gave this advice, under the name of Polly Resolute, to an eighteenth-century reader:

> I conceive parents' authority can extend no farther than what may contribute to the happiness of their child: When it is carried beyond that, and apparent, that they are governed by *mercenary* views, and not the *happiness* of their child, it undoubtedly is laudable in any lady, to avoid the yoke that is preparing for her, by making herself happy in the possession of a man, whose affections and endearing behaviour, is far more to be wished for, than five thousand per annum with one she could never love.

Americans chose their mates as they would, and for three hundred years, Europeans stood amazed. An Austrian visitor in 1842 remarked, "A very remarkable custom in the United States gives girls the freedom to choose a husband according to their fancy; practice does not permit either the mother or the father to interfere in this important matter."

Freedom of choice, however, did not mean freedom of behavior, and the old temptations aroused by bundling reared their seductive heads during the courtship period again and again. There has never been any social support for premarital sex until, possibly, the 1960s, although an eighteenth-century Harvard debating society did consider the question "Whether it be Fornication to lye with ones Sweetheart (after Contraction) before Marriage." One way of combating the sexual urge toward the partner intended for marriage was to encourage short engagements. Despite such precautions, there have always been a substantial number of pregnant brides at American weddings. One set of statistics locates the greatest numbers in the late eighteenth century, during the cultural upheaval following the American Revolution, and in the early 1960s, just before birth-control pills put the whole question in another perspective.

In the nineteenth century, when the statistically lowest number of premarital pregnancies occurred, the internalized restraint imposed on themselves by a courting couple was reinforced by society's ever-vigilant eye. In some places, a single kiss between a man and a "nice girl" committed him to marriage, and pretty surely no nice girl admitted that she had been kissed before she was engaged. In Indiana in 1890, "a 'well-brought-up' boy and girl were commonly forbidden to sit together in the dark," and buggy riding, almost the only recreation a couple could engage in outside the family circle, could only be undertaken with safety for a girl's reputation in daylight. After half-past eight at night, no ride could take place without a chaperon. These rigorous standards for courting were mainly upheld to protect females, whose sole capital in the marriage market (when they no longer brought dowries) was their virginal condition. The double standard, by which men were allowed, or even supposed, to be sexually experienced was probably operative in the cities and in the raw areas of the frontier—Denver in the 1870s had such a sophisticated red-light district that some brothel inmates, much in demand, got thirty dollars a customer—but most of the inhabitants of the country expected only clean-living men to court their girls. Dr. Benjamin Spock and Adlai Stevenson have allowed that they were virgins in their mid-twenties when their marriages took place, in the 1920s, and neither man was from an unsophisticated background. When Dr. Alfred Kinsey of Indiana University made his celebrated study of sexual mores in the 1940s, 80 percent of the men interviewed said they had had some premarital sexual experience, but by that time the United States had participated in two world wars, and, in the words of the song, "How 'ya gonna keep 'em down on the farm after they've seen Paree?"

In the United States, the basis for serious courting—that is, spending time together with intentions of finding a marriage partner—has been called romantic love since the nineteenth century, at least. The opportunity of free choice, so widespread since the earliest days, left room for few other criteria. *Middletown*, the extensive sociological study of Muncie, Indiana, done in 1925, remarked, "Most of Middletown stumbles upon its partners in marriage guided chiefly by 'romance.' Middletown adults appear to regard romance in marriage as something which, like their religion, must be believed in to hold society together. . . . 'You'll know when the right one comes along,' [children] are told with a knowing smile."

But under frontier conditions, love was often ignored or determined by sore necessity. Dakota Territory men staking claims on government land in the 1880s sent for mail-order brides and "married anything that got off the railroad." In his documentary novel about his family's pioneer life, *The Grandmothers*, Glenway Westcott tells of a great-aunt who had married a doctor forty years her senior in Missouri just before the Civil War in order to remove the financial burden of her support from a widowed mother. When the doctor, a Union sympathizer, was shot in his bed by Southern sympathizers, his wife had only one way to escape the same fate. She went up to a wagon driver who was going North.

"You are Mr. Cleaver?"
He breathed heavily through his mouth and nodded.
"You are going north?"
"In the morning."
The most important question was the hardest to ask: "Are you going alone? Are you married?"
"All alone. No, not married."

And so, to avoid the sin of making a journey alone with a strange man, she married him for the ride.

In more recent times and under less harsh conditions, "love" tends to be sparked by proximity. Coed college classmates turn into sweethearts and mates. Neighbors fulfill dreams. Two sociologists did a study of proximity in Seattle in 1961 and discovered that most marriage licenses were granted to engaged men and women living within half a mile of each other. Another sociologist commented on this: "Romeo's love flashed into his life like a bolt of lightning, and young lovers to this day believe that the same thing has happened to them. It is odd, however, that this lightning should fall so often on the girl next door."

The so-called sexual revolution, which began in the 1920s with the increased mobility and privacy offered by the automobile, and escalated sharply in the 1960s, when "the pill" became a common contraceptive device, has affected courting in ways we cannot imagine. From the nineteenth century, when a man could simply show up on Sunday afternoon to pay a call or go buggy riding and his mere presence made his honorable intentions clear, we have come full circle; today, a man can simply approach a woman—or vice versa—at a party, a singles' bar, or a college dance and, in few words, make what our ancestors would have considered his extremely dishonorable intentions clear. When dating replaced courting (the word "dating" became popular in 1920), more sexual experimentation, from flirting to intercourse, became possible. Now every type of social and sexual behavior outside of marriage can occur with relatively little social stigma for the parties involved. But most men and women in their twenties today, it is safe to say, still see some kind of sustained relationship with another individual of the opposite sex as their ultimate social goal. Getting to this goal may involve more experimenting than flirting, but once a partner is fixed on, there follows a period of wooing before the commitment to a long-term association is made. Courting is as good a term as any for that tentative and golden time. An article in *The New York Times* in 1972 on the new sexual freedom pointed out that half of the sexually experienced teenagers interviewed said they intended to marry their lovers. We are back at Harvard College in 1775—"Whether it be Fornication to lye with ones Sweetheart . . . "—the temptations are bound by the expectation of permanence. Whether playing the piano in the parlor or experimenting in a coed dorm, Americans for three hundred years have been making themselves agreeable to the one and only who would make life worth living.

(41) *When, in earlier days, a suitor was recognized as such, he paid his lady many small attentions: Helping her, encumbered with parasol, hat, and gloves, into a boat was one. Nevertheless, the books warned a girl, "Never join in any rude plays that will subject you to being kissed or handled in any way by gentlemen."*

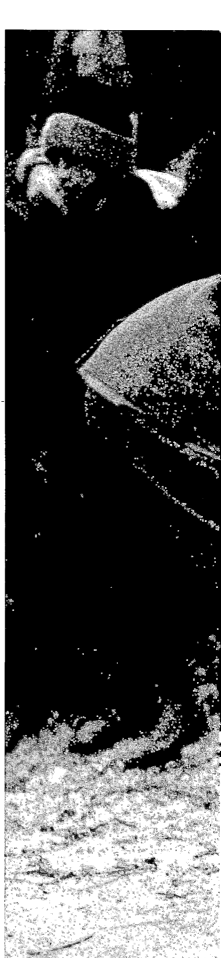

42

(42) *The desolation of the nineteenth-century woman without a man was mimed by these ladies, who weep into their handkerchiefs until their lives are brightened by a chuck under the chin. The men, at least, saw things this way.* (43) *Allowing your skates to be put on by a beau's cold-numbed fingers and then a discreet touch through the gloves as you whirled, arm in arm, around the ice was perfectly permissible.* 43

44

45

(44) *"Making your own fun" was the innocent term applied to any courting activity at home, other than games or "sparking." Music was popular before the radio, and the movies provided packaged entertainment, but the pleasure of singing cannot completely account for this 1915 Oregon couple's exuberance.* (45) *The most deeply felt intimacy does not always occur in private. At the Thompson residence in Lewiston, Montana, in 1905, a man and his fiancée tenderly held hands in the midst of his formidable, well-fed family.*

46

47

Dating replaced courting after World War I. (46) *A Mississippi couple made a date for Saturday night when they met shopping that same afternoon in the 1930s. Things had become more casual, but the element of decorum is still apparent in the woman's straight stance and the distance between the two.* The automobile became the mobile den of vice or liberty, depending on your age, for young people in the 1920s. (47) *The couple who watched a horse race in 1919 are still outside the car and attended by a chaperon, but by 1954* (48) *the versatility of back seats had become appreciated.*

48

50

Habits die hard, and different kinds of accepted social behavior often overlap in the same generation. While some couples were courting in the car quite freely, others stayed at home in the parlor, where the pursuit of happiness could lead only so far. The pictures on the wall of this Polish immigrant home in Buffalo, New York, symbolize the restraints many young people still felt in the 1940s (49). (50) Bill and his fiancée, Joanne, a Chattanooga, Tennessee, pair, were probably no happier in 1971 than the couple holding hands on the Montana porch in 1905 (45), but they're free of corsets and hats and they're free to display their delight in each other more openly.

Families Forming

The creation of a new family means the creation of a new world for the man and woman who undertake to make a home together and, usually, beget children. The redefinition of yourself in terms of the new relationship can mean an almost total rethinking of your life. No longer are you a free, wage-earning worker who has no one to account to and who can think of family as a backdrop and a refuge in times of emergency. After marriage, "family" means a man and woman's daily experience of each other, an experience that they are responsible for making positive. According to two contemporary sociologists, Peter L. Berger and Hansfried Kellner, "Marriage in our society is a *dramatic* act in which two strangers come together and redefine themselves. . . . in our mobile society the significant conversation of the two partners previous to the marriage took place in social circles that did not overlap. With the dramatic redefinition of the situation brought about by marriage, however, all significant conversation for the two new partners is now centered in their relationship with each other." Given the social and geographical mobility of American life, new families are thrown much upon themselves, and the first days, months, and years of marriage have always been a building experience.

The first thing to be built in the past, of course, was literally a place to live. Even in periods of prosperity when there was little pressure to go West and start a new homestead, if a newly married couple remained with the groom's parents, likely as not a new wing would be added to the farmhouse for them. Then, in turn, when the young couple had children of their own, the older generation might move into the wing and turn over the main part of the house to the growing family. Such Pennsylvania-German religious sects as the Amish still live that way, and their farmhouses are a series of sections attached side by side like a set of Chinese boxes. But whether the new home was attached to a family house or was a new bungalow farther along Main Street or a raw cabin in the woods, young couples expected until World War I that the man would already have provided a place to live before the marriage. Often a woman's answer to a rash proposal would be, "When you've got a house, I'll think about it." In the personal reminiscences of growing up on the prairies that she conceived as children's books, Laura Ingalls Wilder described the proposal of marriage she received in 1884. After a certain number of Sunday afternoon buggy rides, her husband-to-be said:

> "I was wondering if you would like an engagement ring."
> "That would depend on who offered it to me," Laura told him.
> "If I should?" Almanzo asked.
> "Then it would depend on the ring," Laura answered and drew her hand away. . . .
> "How do you like this one?" . . .
> "It is a beautiful ring," Laura said. "I think . . . I would like to have it."
> "Then leave it on. It is yours and next summer I will build a little house in the grove on the tree claim. It will have to be a little house. Do you mind?"
> "I have always lived in little houses. I like them."

So necessary was a proper home for a young married couple thought to be that the nation was scandalized in the 1830s and 1840s when setting up housekeeping in boardinghouses became a widespread practice among city newlyweds. It was cheaper for a middle-class couple to have a single room in a boardinghouse than to keep an establishment of their own with the requisite number of servants, and there

(51) *Leonard Dakin captured the sense of wonder a new baby can inspire in a family*
when he photographed his wife holding their son, Roland, in Cherry Valley, New York,
in 1890. Dakin's father and brother regard the new generation.

was a period when 70 percent of the American population could say they had lived at least for a time in boardinghouses, either as unmarried workers away from home or when they were just married. But it was thought immoral for a woman to sit in idleness in a boardinghouse parlor all day. Even if she had servants to do all the work, a proper wife was supposed to have an establishment of her own to manage. A colloquial expression for getting married in the nineteenth century was "to go to housekeeping," and even today one of the objections to people getting married while they are still in college is that they will not have a "real" home maintained by one or both of their earnings. For middle-income Americans who are over college age when they marry, proving that they can establish a home often leads to life-long mortgages.

All of these new possessions require joint decisions, and from the engagement ring onward (Laura Ingalls reserved her decision until she saw the ring) there may be conflict and disillusionment. The expectation of romance that steers many Americans into marriage can be rudely frustrated by the realities of sharing a bankbook and bathroom. Finding that your spouse is accustomed to leaving the "heel" on the cut bread to keep the loaf fresh, whereas you always eat the heel first as a treat, can seem an irreconcilable difference in a cumulative series of clashing habits. A new husband may resent the financial drain a nonworking wife presents; the wife in that situation may resent her financial dependence. Even sexual relations can be an area of conflicting expectations—and were particularly so in former days—although probably no bride in the 1930s was truly as naive as the one referred to in the Thurber cartoon from that period in which one matron says to another, "He proposed something on their wedding night her own brother wouldn't have suggested." In the nineteenth century—and indeed until twenty-five years ago—a man was usually acknowledged master of his house, and this meant that a bride was trying to learn a new job under the eye of a constantly watchful employer whose presence was guaranteed for life. The bride's performance determined her whole future life, and we find poignant today those old jokes about "bride's biscuits" heavy enough for a doorstop and served with silverware from which she has neglected to wash the polish.

In Sinclair Lewis's *Main Street*, his exposé novel of small-town narrowness and hypocrisy, written in 1920, the heroine, Carol Kennicott, meets and marries her doctor husband in her father's home in a large Middle-Western city. When Carol returns to Gopher Prairie, her husband's town, she is appalled by the narrowness of his interests and his friends' lives. But in 1920 there was little opportunity for a woman to discuss her problems with her "breadwinner," who had to deal with the outside world of jobs and farming and finance in order to support both of them. In American society before World War II, understanding a married partner's point of view was less important than maintaining a home. "A high degree of companionship is not regarded as essential for marriage. There appears to be between Middletown husbands and wives of all classes when gathered together in informal leisure-time groups relatively little spontaneous community of interest," declared the 1925 sociological study. In those days, however, as long as there were several families together, a communal moral climate, community pressure gave a newly married pair standards and expectations of success that held them together. Edith Wharton, writing of old New York society of the 1870s, said of a newly married couple in *The Age of Innocence*: "If, now and then, during their travels, they had fallen slightly out of step, harmony had been restored by their return to the conditions she was used to. He had always foreseen that she would not disappoint him, and he had been right. . . . She had represented [for him] peace, stability, comradeship, and the steadying sense of an unescapable duty." Today, social pressure to make a new marriage "work" has diminished; there are fewer outside observers and more conflicting expectations, but perhaps the greater number of alternatives open to contemporary young people before marriage makes them more adaptable to each other in a newly married state.

Whatever the conflicts of the new couple, their resolution may be forced, or interrupted, or postponed by the birth of a child. This, again, required a severe adjustment for the emerging family and may present another contrast between the expectation of bliss and the realization of nuisance. If a newly married pair are very much in love and have resolved their conflicts in the new world that they inhabit, a child may be emotionally superfluous. Freud himself said that "when a love-relationship is at its height, no room is left for any interest in the surrounding world: The pair of lovers are sufficient unto themselves, do not even need the child they have in common to make them happy." A first child makes a difference in the daily life of the couple that is more marked than the change in their lives when they married. A new wife or husband has, for instance, more social options in some areas than she or he had before marriage. The newlywed has added his spouse's friends, hobbies, and contacts to his own. But after the baby comes, all that drops by the wayside. A husband may be a permanent date for the movies, but the arrival of a baby means that neither goes to the movies at all. The fact that the sacrifice is well worthwhile makes it none the less noticeable. Also, children today are almost purely a responsibility, whereas on the old-time farms, they were a welcome addition that would very soon be useful. In the nineteenth century a barren woman felt that she had failed her husband economically as well as emotionally (men were rarely held responsible for the inability to have a child). Today, if children are not felt to be an outright burden, they are undertaken as a care.

Although the arrival of a child may be the most momentous event of the young couple's first years, deciding whether to have it or not is a fairly recent option. Birth control as a possibility, let alone a subject of controversy, has a very sporadically documented history. It was mentioned in ancient writings and practiced in the Renaissance, but it seems that, despite the educated minority's sophistication, ignorance of birth control was the rule for centuries. *Middletown* quotes working-class women who in 1925 had no idea, or only the foggiest one, that birth control was possible. Their reactions to it ranged from disapproval—"God punishes people who deliberately try not to have children"—to a vigorous regret that it was not widely known.

> My daughter and her husband—he's a machinist—didn't know anything about birth control, and they had a second baby and then she insisted that they keep apart until his work was regular enough to support a larger family. He wouldn't and she left him and came home to us here [the speaker had seven children]. . . . I certainly believe in birth control! But I don't know anything about it. I never even heard of it until a little while ago. I sure wish I had known of it when I was young, for then he wouldn't be slaving away to support this big family and my daughter wouldn't be in all the trouble she's in.

This poignant statement was made by an intelligent woman who was trapped both by her ignorance and changing social conditions that made a big family—conceived, literally, for the farm—a burden on a mill worker's salary.

In America in the early days, knowledge of birth control seems to have been sparse. Historian Mary Cable quotes the diary of Governor William Bradford of the Plymouth Colony, who tells of a minister in the 1630s who "overcame" a young woman and, "though he satisfied his lust on her, yet he endeavored to hinder conception." According to Cable, the next mention of birth control in American letters occurs in a book published in 1830 by Robert Dale Owen, son of the founder of the utopian community at New Harmony, Indiana, who advocated it. After that, birth control received fitful and covert attention until the Comstock Law, enacted in 1873, classified birth-control information as pornography. Condoms, referred to in writing in the Renaissance, were a custom-made, rich-man's device for brothel use until the mid-nineteenth century, when the vulcanization of rubber made them commercially viable. Their use increased after the army advocated it during World War I. Not until the arrival of "the pill" in the 1960s was virtual freedom from the uncertainty of mechanical devices possible.

The decision to have a child is influenced by such other factors as prosperity and career opportunities. The birth rate dropped sharply—and the age of men and women at marriage rose—during the Depression. In the prosperous 1950s there was a "baby boom," as there had been at the end of World War II, when all the soldiers returned home eager to reestablish an orderly family life for themselves. In 1972, for the first time in its history, the United States had a zero-population-growth rate, which means that just enough children were born to replace the adult population. This very low birthrate was obviously the result of the many new job opportunities for women and the heightened consciousness among women that they did have alternatives to being homemakers.

Pregnancy, a time of hope and worry, was particularly difficult in Victorian America, when the mother had all the natural concern about herself and the coming baby, but at the same time had to remain reticent about it because the Victorian family, especially if children and old maids were part of it, was not supposed to recognize the fact of pregnancy. The cumbersome hoopskirt of the 1860s was invented to disguise the pregnancy of the Empress Eugénie of France, and that awkward garment could be the symbol for the Victorian attitude toward the subject. A lady from Boston tells in her memoirs of the 1890s that it was apparent at her parents' twenty-fifth wedding anniversary party that her mother was expecting another child, but no one would have thought to ask when it was due. The party was planned and executed as though there were no pregnancy to consider, and everybody had to be happily surprised when the baby arrived a scant three days later.

One reason, besides prudery, for the Victorian conspiracy of silence around birth was the realistic fear that something might go wrong. Given a high mortality rate for both mothers and infants, anticipation of the event was as anxious as it was eager. From about the time of the Civil War, births were attended by a doctor rather that a midwife, but they were deeply private and painful, and many deaths occurred nevertheless. Medical aid did not advance far beyond the seventeenth century, when the remedy for labor pains was a powder made from a virgin's hair. In 1853 Queen Victoria took chloroform at the birth of her eighth child, and that popularized the anesthetic, which slowly made its way across the Atlantic.

The hospital birth with use of anesthetics that became popular in the 1930s was a medical improvement in some points of cleanliness and in the prevention of complications, but it made birth impersonal and tended to deprive the mother of her instinctually important first contact with her child. The recently popular "natural childbirth" during which a woman's body functions naturally and the process is facilitated by exercises and watched over by a doctor, is, of course, a sophisticated version of the way children were born during most of the history of humanity. In the old days of country doctors and midwives, babies were delivered as often on kitchen tables as in bed—and sometimes the kitchen table stood on a dirt floor. But as Margaret Mead has pointed out: "No primitive society leaves the mother alone, nor does any leave her alone among strangers. It remains for modern civilization in the isolation of cities and suburbs to leave a woman approaching childbirth all alone." There was familiarity and sometimes even immunity to familiar germs on that kitchen table. Hospitals, however, did reduce the danger of such threats as the terrible puerperal fever that killed one out of ten mothers in the nineteenth century.

After the birth process and recovery, which has varied in length from the few days a poor woman—one hundred years ago or today—could spare from her duties, to the six weeks required by a Victorian lady of fashion, the child and mother were functioning members of the family. The child demands most of the parents' attention. A first child especially brings sleepless nights, unwonted confinement to the home, and terror to the parents who must maintain the fragile life that wails inexplicably at 4:00 A.M. This total reorientation of a relationship that has itself demanded a recent adjustment from the premarried state can be severely trying. Parents feel that they are in a combat zone, and they sustain wartime stresses. They can become irritable and tenacious of their rights and unable to see the light at the end of the tunnel. Some of our photographs hint at when the first glimpse of that light may come: when a nursing baby looks its mother square in the eye; or when a young uncle, ninety years ago, looked enviously over the porch rail at his small nephew, secure in its mother's lap and love; or when another baby, sixty years ago, was dandled and bounced and held by everyone and snapped by his only slightly bigger brother's camera; or when little Southern children peered through steamy windows at their new sibling, lying in clean, worn blankets in an orange crate. At some point there is the realization, fleeting at first, behind clouds of concerns, that this baby and its parents are a unit unto themselves. They are more than three people. They are a family.

(52) The baby and mother who were photographed at bath time in Wisconsin in the 1890s show the same feelings a modern mother and child might. The mother was less secure in her happiness, however; more than one baby out of every ten born between 1890 and 1900 died before it was one year old.

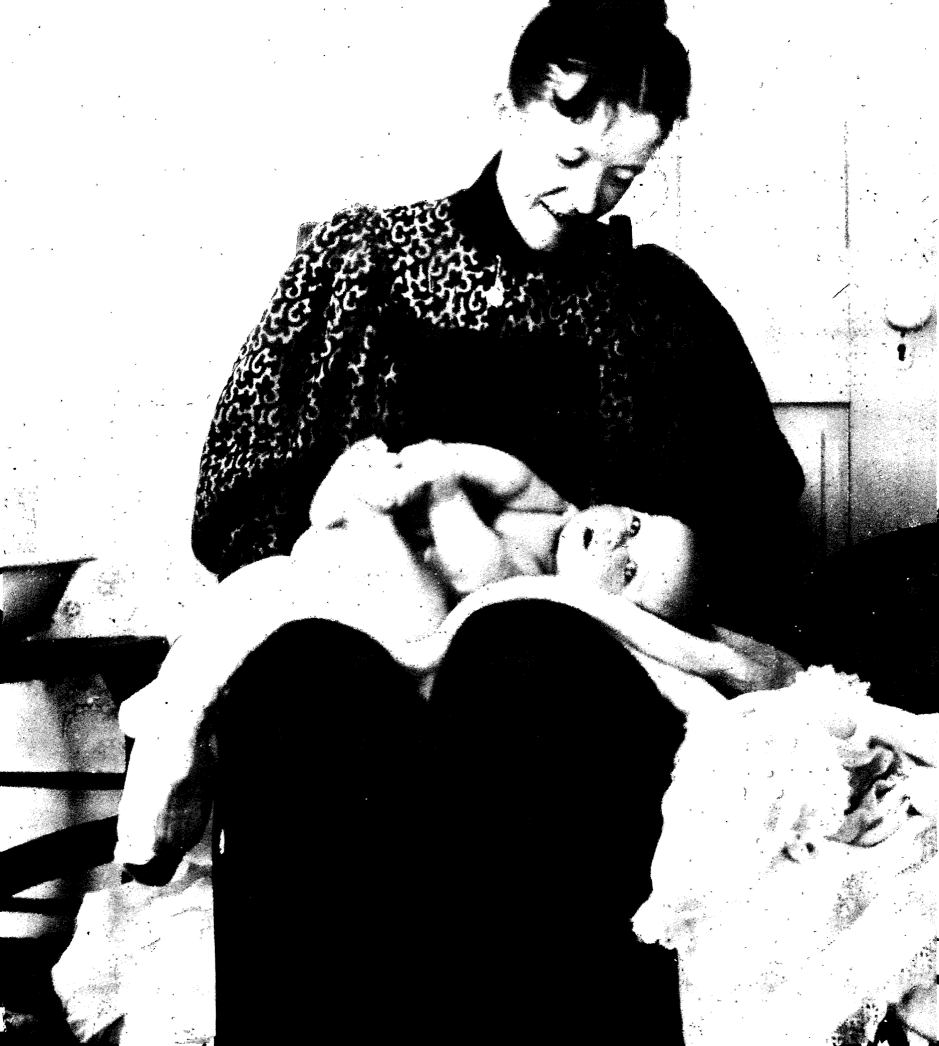

(53) *Mrs. Morgan of Hanover, New Hampshire, proud mother of a son, Norman, born April 13, 1919, kept a "baby book" of snapshots just like the millions that were made after the Brownie camera appeared in the early 1900s. Norman's grandfather held him for the photographer at six weeks, his aunt at eight weeks, and his mother at ten weeks; finally, his brother snapped Norman at eight months. A declining infant mortality rate may have helped parents see their babies as little people with personalities of their own. (Before the twentieth century, a mother was often fearful of becoming too attached to her baby because it was so likely to die.) (54) This little Oregon boy in 1915 gave a rare and tender sibling's welcome to the family's new baby.*

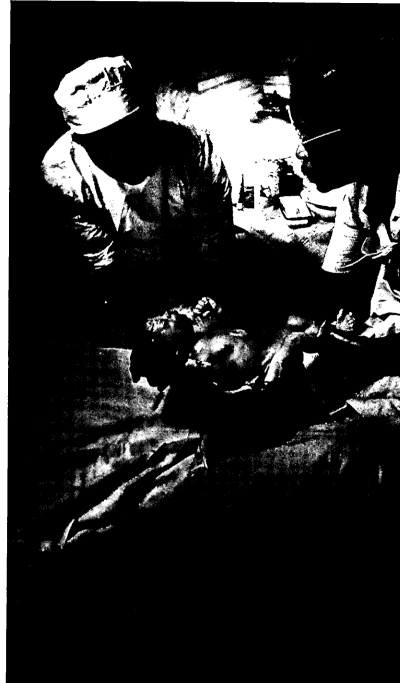

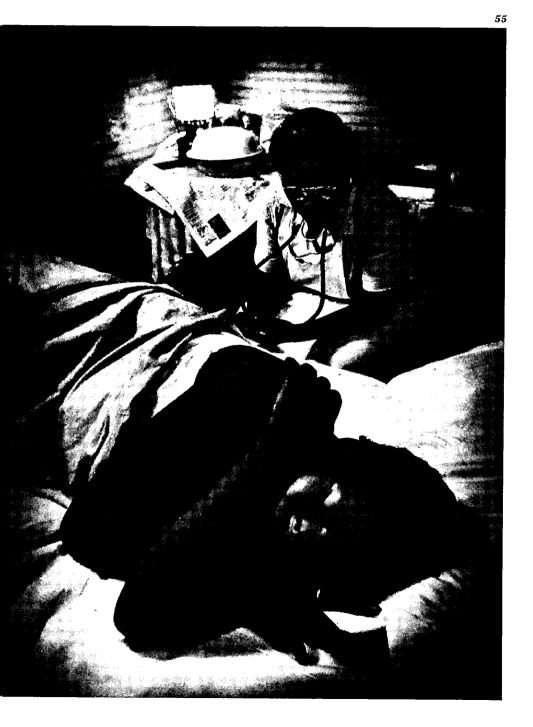

(55–57) *Maude Callen, a nurse-midwife in South Carolina in the 1940s, delivered this baby in a rural house the way babies had been delivered for thousands of years. Today, about eighty percent of the world's babies are still delivered by midwives. It was said of a retired midwife that in the old days, "If families were in real bad shape about something to eat, she'd take sweet potatoes and milk and butter in her saddle bags." After she had delivered the baby and cooked the family a meal, she would wrap the new arrival in clean rags and lay him in his orange-crate crib, where his brothers and sisters could peep at him through the window.*

57

58

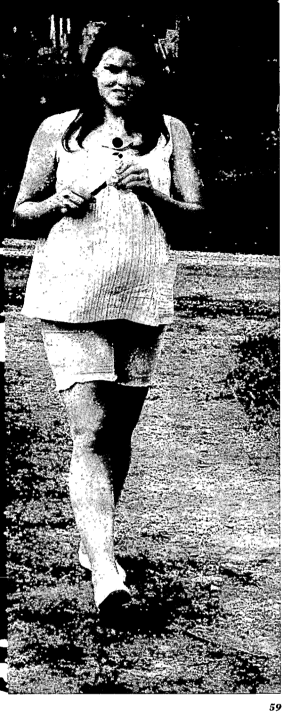

59

(58–60) *The joy of pregnancy usually compensates for the nuisance of morning sickness or fear of the hospital. When a woman feels herself growing like a ripening plant in the earth, she wants her husband to share the sensual pleasure of new life.*

60

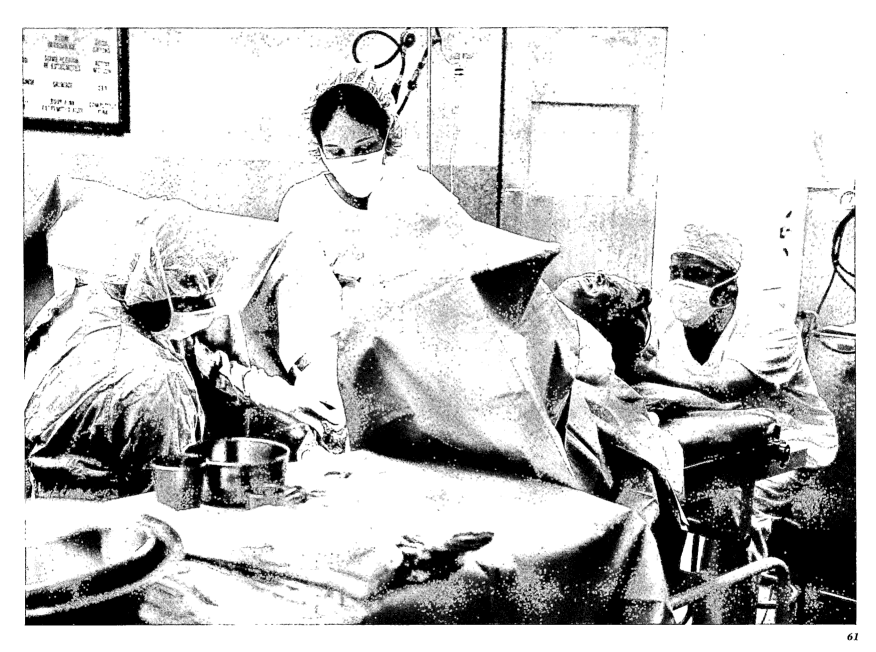

61

(61, 62) *Parents who have taken natural-childbirth*
classes often can remain together during the birth.
With a minimum of drugging and artificial
stimulation, the mother times her labor contractions.
Her husband beside her, as in this picture of a 1974
Connecticut birth, she participates fully in the
triumphant emergence of a new being, who stretches
his arm out (62) *to greet the world. The need to force a*
baby to breathe is usually the result of the mother's
anesthetization.

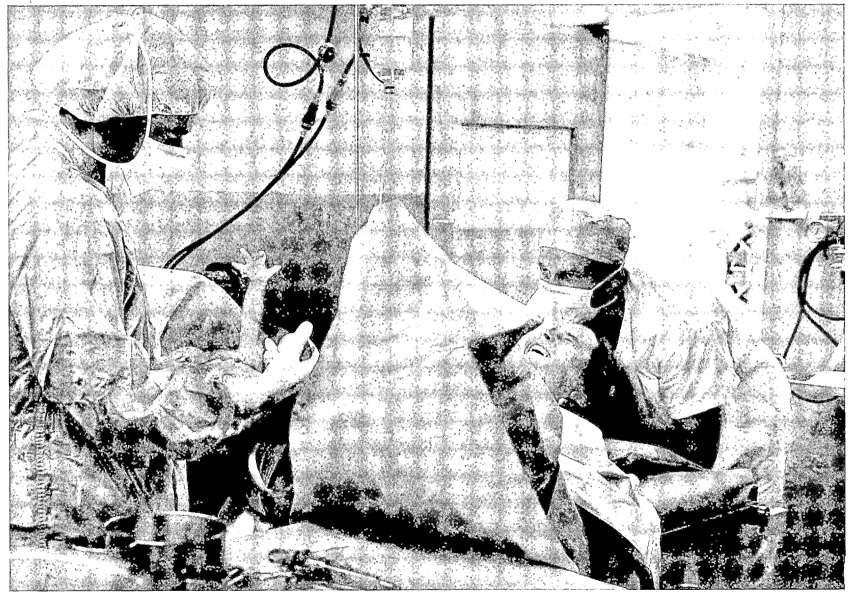

The family's members who were around before the new baby came have to adjust in different ways. *The father* (63), proud of a new child of his flesh and blood, loses sleep when the baby cries; then looking to the future, he plans for baseball caps, dance dresses, or college. *An older sister* (64) has to get used to sharing mother and father. *Mother* (65) has to nourish as well as tend the baby, who here casts a wary eye on the food source. Everyone is aware again of being more than an individual; they are members of the family team.

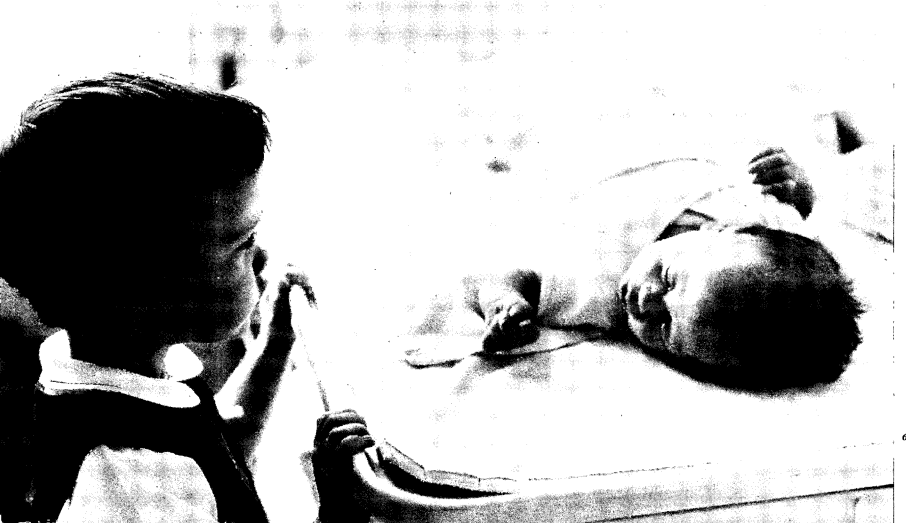

(66) *In 1838 French traveler Alexis de Tocqueville called the American log cabin "a little world of its own, an ark of civilization lost in a sea of leaves." The Tidwells' cabin in Sunnyside, Utah, had all the qualities of overcrowding, dirt, and discomfort that made civilization a gallant dream of the future for its inhabitants.*

Home–the Residence

Abraham Lincoln, as we all know, was born in a log cabin. So, for that matter, were Andrew Jackson and Andrew Johnson and James A. Garfield. Herbert Hoover was born in a small frame cabin—almost as good as log for campaign purposes—and William McKinley campaigned for the presidency of the United States from his front porch. This belief in the importance of a president's ties to a particular humble dwelling is called the log-cabin myth; it is unique in world politics, and it has obviously been strong enough in America to affect the highest political office. There is good reason for linking our origins, national as well as personal, with a single small house.

For many Americans growing up in the rural nineteenth and early twentieth centuries, the home and the family it contained was the strongest social unit they knew. Frederick Jackson Turner, the historian whose 1893 "frontier theory" maintained that the opportunities of the frontier had decisively shaped American character, declared, "Complex society is precipitated by the wilderness into a kind of primitive organization based on the family." In other words, on the frontier there may have been rudimentary schools and village councils but they were difficult of access and had a shifting membership; the only form of government that every person was involved in every day was the government of Ma and Pa at home. That government could be severe: Marguerite Noble, an Arizona schoolteacher, remembers her pioneer father as "an old-time Texas cattleman, [who] had his shortcomings, among them his belief that women were little more then serfs. . . . We accepted his tenet and discipline." The seat of this family government, in which parents—or, more likely, one parent—had the power of shaping lives and building immortal souls, was often the log cabin, a rough hut assembled from felled tree trunks with the bark still on them.

From the caveman's shelter to the pioneer's cabin—ten thousand years had seemingly advanced domesticity hardly at all. But in America the slight difference between a cave and a cabin was of immense significance; whereas the caveman had crawled into the first natural shelter he could find, the pioneer, bringing with him some notion of man's ability to determine his own fate, created a shelter, however rude, in defiance of nature.

Those log shelters were rude indeed, make no mistake. The first ones in America were Scandinavian peasant huts put up by Swedish immigrants along the Delaware River in the seventeenth century. The Puritans in New England, not having come from such a freely wooded country as Sweden, had never heard of log cabins and made even more primitive mud-and-wattle shelters from clay and twigs. From those simple seventeenth-century buildings to the sod houses that the Plains settlers put up in the 1880s, many American homes had dirt floors, with the snow and rain blowing through their walls and a fire barely heating one corner when it wasn't threatening to burn down the house. Hamlin Garland, writing of the Middle-Western plains in the nineteenth century, remembered: "Winter! No man knows what winter is until he has lived through it in a pine-board shanty on a Dakota plain with only buffalo bone for fuel."

But there was a further difference between the cave and the cabin made by those people who centered their lives in their one log room. The cabin was a dwelling wrested from nature; it represented an act of choice and will, and the choice extended to a deliberate maintenance of culture, however crude the surroundings. In 1835 Alexis de Tocqueville, visiting America from France, found a log cabin in Ohio surprising.

> We went into the log house; the inside was quite unlike that of the cottages of European peasants;
> there was more that was superfluous and fewer necessities; a single window with a muslin curtain;
> on the hearth of beaten earth a great fire which illuminated the whole interior; above the hearth a
> good rifle, a deerskin, and plumes of eagles' feathers; to the right of the chimney a map of the United

States, raised and fluttering in the draft from the crannies in the wall; near it, on a shelf formed from a roughly hewn plank, a few books, a Bible, the first six cantos of Milton, and two plays of Shakespeare; there were trunks instead of cupboards along the wall; in the center of the room, a rough table with legs of green wood with the bark still on them, looking as if they grew out of the ground on which they stood; on the table was a teapot of English china, some silver spoons, a few cracked teacups, and newspapers.

The hearth of beaten earth was what human beings had lived on since they crept out of the caves; otherwise, this cabin was unique to a nation who thought of themselves as independent yeomen, with each family its own unit of government and culture, reading Shalespeare in the wilderness.

Log-cabin families were also small industrial plants. Until the mid-nineteenth century, most of the necessities of life were made at home. Beside a cabin in the woods, filling up the clearing and straggling away among the stumps, there would be a smokehouse for curing meat; a spring house, where crocks of butter and other perishables could be kept in the cool water from the spring; and an iron "bilin'" pot in which clothes and slaughtered hogs were indiscriminately washed. There would also be an "ash hopper"—a contraption for running water over wood ashes to make lye for homemade soap—and, of course, pens for all the barnyard animals—chickens, pigs, goats, and geese—whose flesh and fur and feathers fed and clothed the family. Because everything that had to be done was started from scratch and not much could be saved up (Mason jars permitting home-canning were not invented until 1858), each day had a full complement of chores for every member of the family. Everyone was much closer to the sources of food and comfort than people were in even the late nineteenth century, and when dark came at night it was the total encompassing dark of the country—only relieved by a wood fire that had itself to be contrived with much laborious hewing and chopping.

Given such a hard-won existence, wrested from the surrounding forest, the wonder is not that the log cabin was so primitive but that it was so refined. It represented the only hold on civilization its owners had, and sometimes that hold was precarious. A traveler from St. Louis found more casual intimacy than he cared for when spending the night in a backwoods Missouri cabin in 1847. When it was bedtime, "the old man stripped unscrupulously and sought his share of the one collapsed-looking pillow, and the sons cavalierly followed his example, leaving the old woman, the gals, and the stranger to settle any question of delicacy that might arise." There was no privacy, and the frontiersman went in and out of his cabin as thoughtlessly as he went in and out of his clothes. If an Englishman's home was his castle, an early nineteenth-century American's was an extension of his very body.

Just how drastically the inventions of the late nineteenth and early twentieth centuries changed home life can be pretty well understood by making a partial list of them. Before 1850 people lived much as they had for five thousand years before, as far as growing food, carrying water, and making fires went; after 1850 American families had sewing machines (1850); telephones (1876); electric light (1879); motion pictures—important as a source of entertainment outside the home (1891); automobiles; cash-and-carry economy stores (1912) and self-service stores (1916); mail-order houses—which made other inventions available to the farmer (1872); "rural free delivery" of mail—which made the mail-order houses practicable (1893); streetcars (1850s)—these made suburbs possible, which in turn increased the size of cities dramatically; Clarence Birdseye's frozen foods (1929)—which made fresh vegetables available all year round and revolutionized American eating habits; and paper bags (1860). The list could go on and on, but try imagining life without any of the above-mentioned items.

One of the most important inventions affecting domestic life was the development in the 1830s of the balloon-frame house. Most older wooden houses in our cities today were built with the device: A framework of two-by-four planks made for each wall was raised into place; clapboards were nailed across the outside, laths and plaster put on the inside. The balloon frame could not have come about without power-driven saws; after its appearance a man no longer had to spend months constructing a unique, immovable dwelling from the ground up. A balloon frame could be put together in a few days by professional carpenters using premade plans, and the framework could be raised in one day and covered in a week. The balloon frame did not gain universal acceptance right off—its name came from the jeering taunt that the framework would blow away like a balloon with the first gust of wind—but after it caught on, homes were easier to construct, and their construction was less the individual owner's effort and more a standardized product. From the balloon frame to the first machine-made collar buttons of the 1840s, home life was tied with many new threads to town and factory.

Despite the new links between the home and the store, which broke down the economic self-sufficiency of a house or farmstead, American homes were still self-sufficient social units until World War I. Family members found their amusement in each other. The front porch, seen at the time through a veil of honeysuckle or Dutchman's-pipe and remembered through a haze of nostalgia, is evidence that folks spent their leisure time at home. Women in small towns, even those who had no help and might have spent a morning scrubbing clothes up and down a washboard, got dressed up in an "afternoon" dress and sat on the porch sewing after their noontime dinner. People sang on front porches in the evenings, and the preliminary stages of courtship went on in the shadows behind the vine on the front porch.

The later, more serious stages of courtship flowered in the parlor, and the very presence of a parlor in almost every American house built between 1850 and 1915 testifies to the importance of the home as the scene of family rituals. The parlor was decorated and closed off, to be dusted and used once a week when a suitor came or when the family, slipping off the horsehair sofa, sat for a stiff and decorous hour on Sunday afternoon in unaccustomed idleness. Russell Lynes said in *American Heritage* (October 1963): "It is not surprising that in a society that was restless, ambitious, and materialistic the parlor—which represented calm, dignity, continuity, and culture—should have been set aside, its double doors firmly shut." The parlor was a sanctuary, kept for proposals of marriage, weddings, and funerals. Of all the principal domestic events, only birth happened elsewhere—upstairs in the great, heavy family bed.

The ornamentation of the primitive home-shelter received a boost with the industrial prosperity of the East after the Civil War. The urge to deck the parlor with antimacassars and the porch with jigsaw-tortured wood ran riot in the mansions of new industrial millionaires. Fifth Avenues in Pittsburgh and New York and the waterfront in Newport were lined with gross marble chateaux and castles and "cottages" that still had little or no plumbing. Toilets drained into a pipe, the only air vent from which gave into the master bedroom. Sewer gas, thought to be a hazard of poverty living, poisoned the rich as well.

Finally after World War I, a flurry of such home improvements as electricity for light and power and gas for cooking came along concurrent with new diversions outside the home and reduced the home's importance in family life. Women and children no longer needed to spend so much time at chores; they were free to go out, and the movies made a reason and Ford a means for doing so. Parlors declined in importance; by the middle 1920s, the parlors in old houses were being turned into "living rooms," and they weren't built into new houses at all. Nobody courted in the parlor anymore; they "necked" in a car or drove to a public dance hall. Hospital births replaced home births, and funeral parlors deprived the home parlor of one more raison d'être.

Along with the loss of domestic functions to the outside world, the home received the communication lines of telephone, radio, and eventually television. The family had still more alternatives to looking at each other's faces around the lamplit sitting-room table. After the dinner dishes were washed (a chore that remained a chore for some years), big sister could go talk to her friends on the telephone instead of having to talk to little sister or grandma—who probably didn't live with the family by this time, anyway. Ironically, the new communication lines reduced communication within the family. Each family member listened to radio or watched television as an individual, in the same way, essentially, that people watch movies; and the telephone confirmed family members in their community peer-group allegiance. What a father told his teenage son about drinking or smoking pot—to take extreme examples—could be contradicted by the son's friends half an hour later over the upstairs phone dragged into the son's bedroom for the purpose, with the door closed dramatically on the cord.

In this modern family, sitting in their single-family house, with their minds ranging away from the dinner table to outside concerns, like birds sharing a perch, each looking out for his own worm, the one isolated member who didn't have outside concerns was likely to be the mother. The adjunct to the new, smooth-running house that is used primarily as a nighttime perch is the frustrated housewife.

Because the house could be taken care of efficiently by one person, the wife and mother of a family was left in charge of things. Immured in her home, the housewife found that the house was considered to require her total attention but not necessarily anyone else's. Fathers worked at jobs that indirectly maintained the family by means of a paycheck, and the children worked at school, but nobody except the mother worked directly *for* the family—washing, cooking, and housecleaning. The mother as chauffeur, cook, gardener, and drudge was a product of the middle decades of the twentieth century. Before 1920 everyone drudged; after 1960 household chores began to be split between husbands and wives. These are vast oversimplifications, of course, but in terms of broad general trends, that was what happened.

Because for the first time in history the direct labor of most family members was not required to maintain their living place, homes were taken more casually. They could be acquired more casually than ever before, too, with mortgages and partial payments. *Middletown* reported that in 1890, "a young man of good character with $350 in cash" could not buy a $750 building lot, but in 1925 everybody had a mortgage from the building-and-loan association. Industry moved its management-level employees around so often that children were likely to live in three or four different houses while they were growing up. It was in the 1920s that Emily Post, the *doyenne* of American etiquette, said significantly that it was more acceptable in good society to refer to a building where a family other than your own lived as the So-and-sos' "house," not their "home."

Yet the shared dwelling is one of the strongest indicators that a group of people are a family. And if the only association people have in that dwelling is around the dinner table or watching TV for an hour, they have occasionally felt the urge, while moving from ranch house to duplex, to recreate the old conditions of the shared home life. In a contemporary novel, Diane Johnson describes the Fry family, "a curious mixture of contemporary sophistication and farmy anachronism. Their house is an example of this. It is one of the best all-electric, built-in-kitchen California kind, in which Mother Fry's Duncan Phyfe looks uncomfortable, and she keeps trying to grow tulips and lilacs outside it, like an Englishwoman who refuses to give in to India."

To the degree that such harkening-back to pioneer days is artificial, we decry it and are amused at homemade bread cut with an electric breadknife. But pretense can express desire, and the desire for the shared experience of building a home is primeval and surely worthy.

The shared experience of a bathroom that several people want to use at once and the shared experience of chaos in the kitchen at six o'clock, when the children are home from school and the father is home from work and the mother is trying to get dinner, constitute the irreducible grounds of life together that modern conveniences cannot decant away. Probably that is just as well. If sex and eating are basic human drives, so are companionship and intimacy. For modern families that neither plow fields, nor knead bread, nor chop kindling, and whose physical contact may be limited to jostling on the subway or to supervised mayhem on the football field, the shared bathroom and shared exuberance of too many people in too small a kitchen are vital experiences that spark a sense of life.

Homesteads are on the decline, but the log cabins that are the symbolic American home were never homesteads in the rooted, permanent sense. They were just shelters from the elements that protected the flame of family life and civilization despite primitive conditions. The flame still has to be nurtured, children must be cared for, husbands and wives still share beds (or rooms—the twin bed was supposed to be a homewrecker when it first appeared in the 1920s), all under a roof that is still home. The American sense of home has always tended to be in the present tense—where you live now—rather than in the past tense—an ancestral, rooted dwelling. "Home is Where You Hang Your Hat" went a popular song.

If the American interest in the present moment sometimes splits a family asunder, diverting the members off into their business and community preoccupations away from home, that is unfortunate. You can't have everything, and people who live together because they are interested in a present life together can, as often as not, make that life when they are at home very good indeed.

After balloon-frame construction became common, making bigger houses easier to build, rooms began to be assigned different functions; no longer did everyone eat and sleep in one big room. (67) A front porch, such as this Boston family enjoyed in the 1890s, was popular all summer. (68) Different generations would gather to work in the sitting room as the Dakins of Cherry Valley, New York, did in 1880. Family social life centered in and around the house until after World War I.

67

68

69

70

(69) *In the winter most farm people, such as this old Maine couple, spent time in the kitchen where the wood-burning stove kept things reasonably warm. The Sears-Roebuck catalogue, or "wish-book," for 1900 offered a brand-new nickel-plated wood-burning stove for $17.48. This was expensive; a farmer that year would get less than a dollar a bushel for this wheat.* (70) *Pianos were both a status symbol and a real source of entertainment for families, whose main amusement was their own company. The instrument was as expensive, proportionally, as a television would be for a modern family, and it demanded more effort, but, if this upstate New York family is any indication, it gave back good value in fun.* (71) *The dining-room table, under the hanging kerosene lamp, was where the family gathered three times a day for meals that included steak and potatoes and pie for breakfast but no fresh vegetables from October until May. Parties like Captain Barton's in Lawrence, Kansas, in 1905, generated a lot of excitement.*

72

73

74

*Mass production and buying on installments—both of which became widespread in the
1920s—filled American homes with possessions, many of which resembled each other to some
extent. In 1936 Margaret Bourke-White did a photographic essay on Muncie, Indiana, which
had been the subject of the pioneering sociological study* Middletown. *These three
"Middletown" homes reflect lower-, middle-, and upper-class domesticity; the differences
however, lie in the quality of the clutter rather than in the tokens of comfort. The rich mill
owner (72) has a grand piano and crystal candelabra; the working man who has lost his leg
in a mill accident and rents his house for ten dollars a month has more children than
goods (73); Mayor Bunch's wife (74) has collected old American glass. Despite differences,
eighty percent of "Middletown's" families lived in single-family houses with their own yards.*

75

Although home remains the scene of the most spontaneous, habitual socializing that people enjoy, the telephone, the radio, and the television profoundly changed the nature of home life. Today, families are likely to resemble the Texas farm couple of the 1930s (75) who listen in silence to the voice "on the air," rarely entertaining themselves by playing cards at the kitchen table (76) or singing around the piano—if indeed they still have a piano.

77

Eating together can produce a sense of family feeling as well as nourishment. It can also, however, become a draining, repetitive chore for the one who cooks and a confining ritual for younger family members. (77) In the 1960s, a New Jersey grandmother seemed to use mealtime as an opportunity to air her woes, to the evident boredom of the teenage girl at the right. (78) Seven o'clock is the hour of chaos in the kitchen for young mothers like this suburban one of the 1950s, who was photographed hurrying to get the meal for three children under way before the father arrived home from work.

As late as 1936, almost forty percent of the families in one midwestern city had no bathtubs, and nearly twenty percent had only the use of an outdoor privy. By 1960, all but a few Americans had at least one bathroom in their homes; it became the right of every American to deal with dirt and body functions in private in his own home. And yet, as for Tom Duffy, a Wisconsin father of ten (79), privacy is often an illusion. Ironically, modern family members may know each other more intimately than families did in the old days of one-room cabins, when they retired to public baths or the woods. (80) The bedroom in which one is most vulnerable and most intimate with a mate also becomes only relatively secluded as the size of the family increases. A New England lawyer, his wife, and their first child have a moment of Saturday-morning play that makes up in family communication what is lost in connubial privacy.

(81) *Farmer Ethan Blanchard with his wife and son, Achilles, of Mapleton, Utah, posed for the photographer in the middle of their usual work day. Mrs. Blanchard has brought a basket of peaches and a keg of water to the men, who are harvesting the thirteen-acre farm's wheat crop. Ethan holds a scythe with a cradle attached to catch the wheat as it is cut.*

Work

One of the criteria for judging what constitutes a family is economic. In a very practical sense, families are people who have common economic interests and property. This is true today as regards house ownership, stocks, bonds, furniture, and jewelry; and common family economic concerns extend to the cost of rearing and educating children. What is not usually common for the modern family, however, is the work that supports a family.

Until about 1900, most families all over the world worked *together* for their mutual support. Some work, naturally, was apportioned to individual members according to age, ability, or sex: Old people did the spinning and cooking that didn't demand much movement or strength, women tended cattle or gardened, and men did the heavy plowing. But everybody was doing some part of the work needed to maintain the family business—i.e., a farm. It was this joint work enterprise that made large families a positive boon and not the burden they later became. A young couple was likely to stay with one of the parent families until there were children old enough to help with the farm work. Every available hand was needed for the labor on a farm, and family members were regarded as factory hands or even as white-collar employees are today: If they were not actively helping in the work, then they were an encumbrance.

So involved was the earlier family relationship with work that, according to an eighteenth-century quotation used by Edward Shorter in his study of peasant life, "The loss of a stable animal grieves a peasant more than the loss of his wife. The first may only be recuperated with money; the second is repaired with another woman, who will bring with her some money and furniture and who, instead of impoverishing the household, will increase its wealth." The economics of this situation, although perhaps tempered in America, where women tended to be at a premium and were usually more fondly regarded, held good throughout the Western world. You either brought in something for the family or you cost the family something; there was no extra money to permit considerations in between.

What exactly you cost the family varied, but proportionate to income, prices were high even in the late nineteenth century. In 1900 there were nearly twenty-four million men working in this country and nearly eleven million of them were farmers. A wheat crop of sixty bushels in 1880 would bring a market price of fifty dollars. In order to grow that many bushels, a farmer would have to have forty acres under cultivation. The average farm on a rocky New England mountainside was comprised of forty acres. The farms in the West were much larger—some on the Great Plains would become vast—but even so the margin of profit was big enough only for subsistence in many cases. Wages paid to a hired man or money for doctor's bills could mean the difference between paying the taxes or taking out a mortgage.

Before 1880 nearly 40 percent of the farm families in the United States were tenants on other people's land. By the turn of the century, this percentage had decreased, not because more men owned their own farms but because fewer people were farming. Despite the Populist political movement against conglomerates and in defense of the small farmer, the Western farms had become big businesses, run usually by corporations and often employing many more workers than a family could supply. The small farms run by one family had been sabotaged in other ways than by competition with the industrialized farms. The opportunities for independence always made each man value his labor enough to want his own farm, or at least a job with a respectable company. Nobody wanted to remain the hired man or single tenant who was needed on the old small farms.

"I'm going on fourteen," Laura said. "I can help, Pa. I know I can."
    The mowing machine had cost so much that Pa had no money left to pay for help. He could not trade work, because there were only a few homesteaders in this new country and they were busy on their own claims. But he needed help to stack the hay.

"Well," Pa said, "maybe you can. We'll try it. If you can, by George! we'll get this haying done all by ourselves!"

Laura could see that the thought was a load off Pa's mind and she hurried to the shanty to tell Ma.

"Why, I guess you can," Ma said doubtfully. She did not like to see women working in the fields. Only foreigners did that. Ma and her girls were American, above doing men's work. But Laura's helping with the hay would solve the problem. She decided, "Yes, Laura, you may."

This passage from Laura Ingalls Wilder's *The Long Winter* encapsulates the small farmer's experience and dilemma in the 1880s. Mr. Ingalls has taken a large claim of undeveloped land from the government because he needs to harvest a large crop to compete with the big Western farms. The "mowing machine" was a necessity on his enlarged farm, but it "cost so much" that poor Mr. Ingalls, who only has four daughters, cannot hire help. Male children meant the difference between bankruptcy and success on a farm. The system of trading work, which he considers, is as old as European communal farms where a whole village worked the same fields. But that isn't an option either on the American plains, where every man is dazzled by the promise of being his own landowner. The frontier work "bees" in which everyone helped to build everyone else's barns, and quilt their quilts had declined, along with the prospects of the small farm. So Mr. Ingalls is left to depend on the help of his daughters—the only kind his small farm can afford. In Europe the women in a farm family had not been averse to pitching in with the hardest jobs when necessary. But if every American male was his own boss, every American female was a lady, no field-working peasant. So Mr. Ingalls was further hampered here by the feeling that ownership of that farm gave him the status that precluded having his daughters work in the fields.

The European emigrants to the United States who came in the late nineteenth century from southern and eastern Europe had no tradition that excepted women from hard labor and, when they first arrived, they had no aspirations to gentility that might have kept certain members from participating in the family enterprise of keeping afloat. Their place of work, however, was not the open land of the West but the cramped, pestiferous tenements of the cities, notably, New York's Lower East Side. There, for an average wage (in 1900) of $12 a week for the 120 *dozen* kneepants that a family of six and two boarders could turn out in the notorious home sweatshops, the ideal of joint family labor came to an inglorious end. Economically, circumstances were not so different from the farm—everyone was an essential cog in the family wheel of mutual maintenance. In the sweatshops, however, as was not true on many farms, the workers were producing for outside agents, and the work ran counter to the normal domestic routine. On the farm, milking cows and putting in a truck garden brought in money at the market on Saturday and also provided food for the family dinner table every night. In the sweatshops, father, mother, and children down to the age of seven or eight spent twelve or more hours a day sitting cramped in one position cutting cloth and sewing trousers, caps, and coats, or, more cruelly yet, making frivolous artificial flowers or cigars for the middle class to enjoy while the "sweaters" developed tubercular chests and bad eyes. There was no one in a sweatshop family to take care of the baby—for the work required the attention of the adults and older children—or to do more than rudimentary marketing and cooking. On a family-run farm, the schedule was determined by nature and couldn't be hurried, so there was usually time for domestic chores, even when they weren't farm chores.

Wage earning that demanded the whole family's efforts was like rowing a lifeboat: you had to do it or you would sink, but unfortunately, when rescue came in the form of higher wages and more widely spread industry, everyone dispersed, with nothing to show for the past efforts but the fact of survival. This was subtly different from working together on the farms, for the farm itself would survive individual family members and form a common object of attachment and nostalgia, no matter how much effort it had extracted from the family members. Before about 1875, families worked to stay together on the farm (rather than go West, go to the poorhouse, or go into factories); after 1875 many worked to escape their current sweatshop circumstances. This continuing desire to move upward financially could easily carry over into a desire to move upward socially also, and as generations bettered their circumstances in industry there remained only the intangible and shifting bonds of ethnic culture to keep extended families together.

This decentralization of families and the radically changed lifestyles of twentieth-century families are thus the result of the Industrial Revolution of the late nineteenth century—when America changed from a nation with a basically rural population and an agrarian economy to an urban, industrial nation. Those 11 million farmers who constituted nearly half the population in 1900 had largely moved to town by 1925 when the sociological study *Middletown* was done.

A Rip Van Winkle who fell asleep in the Middletown of 1885 to awake today would marvel at the change. . . . In the quiet county-seat of the middle eighties men lived relatively close to the earth and its products. In less than four decades, business class and working class, bosses and bossed, have been caught up by Industry, this new trait in the city's culture that is shaping the pattern of the whole of living.

The authors also observed:

For both working and business class no other accompaniment of getting a living approaches in importance the money received for their work. It is more this future, instrumental aspect of work, rather than the intrinsic satisfactions involved, that keeps Middletown working so hard as more and more of the activities of living are coming to be strained through the bars of the dollar sign. . . . there appears to be a constantly closer relation between the solitary factor of financial status and one's social status.

By the third decade of the twentieth century, many families were more concerned with the income that would permit them to take a prominent place in a consumer society than they were with a mutual effort for a particular goal. The days were gone forever when the whole family would make economic provision for one member at the quite literal expense of the others. In Glenway Westcott's novel *The Grandmothers,* one pioneer farm boy says to his brother: "Besides . . . you hadn't ought to be a singer. Pa's made sacrifices. Only one of us boys could have a chance. I gave up wanting to be a veterinary so you could be a minister." By 1925, work for gain—and as much gain as possible—had replaced work for subsistence.

The new industry and new wages of industry enabled parents to try to give their children things they themselves never had. Their children, in turn, made more money and repeated the process. By the mid-twentieth century, family members were working almost in competition with each other rather than for a common family goal. Middletown working-class mothers said that they would give up food before they would give up the Ford or take the kids out of school—status symbols of equal importance in the mothers' minds. Leaving the kids in school meant that they would get jobs with better incomes or more prestige than their parents had, and the result was often feelings of alienation, expressed rather wistfully by an elderly father in the 1960s: "Well, you've gone much farther than I ever did—you're way beyond me now, but I guess that's the way it's supposed to be. There wouldn't be any progress otherwise." His son had written a book that was well reviewed in *The New York Times;* the father had come from a poor farming background and put himself through college working in steel mills.

The very suburbs that make concentric rings around American cities of all sizes, rippling away from the cities' industrial pools, testify to the separation of work and family life in our society. Although the suburbs are considered a retreat from the grim realities of work in the inner city, they may just as easily be considered a response to the impulse to remove the clutter of home life and untidy emotions from the pure efforts of work with its progress charts and regular wages. Talk to a reasonably successful middle-aged businessman when he is off guard and see whether he regards his home as his spiritual and emotional center or finds his tidy, humming office at the center of his thoughts.

Every member of a family who has his own job—whether it is bringing in the income or going to school—must necessarily develop his interests away from the family's common blood and residence. Working together forges the same bonds of acceptance between people that exist in a family. When families worked together, the bond was doubly strong; today, when family members work separately, the family bond itself is threatened by outside interests.

By the 1960s, families were doing their "jobs"—whatever they were—alone or at least away from the rest of the family. For the most part, only the poor were left in "Pa and Ma" delicatessens and on the land; and in both cases those endeavors were stripped of the dignity that farming and owning a business once had. Only the very rich, sprinkled across the top of city populations, might still have family enterprises that gave them a common identity and common goals. Family feeling—the sense of belonging to a group of people related by blood, who share a name and common characteristics and desires—competes in modern America with peer-group loyalty and work allegiance, and often comes out worsted in the contest. When a stranger joined a party in 1960s America, people would ask about him, "What does he do?" not "Who is he?" as they would have done seventy-five or a hundred years ago, when the answer might have been that he was a so-and-so, a member of one of the families who lived up on top of the hill by the schoolhouse, for instance.

84

(82) *The steel plow was the invention that permitted settlement of the Great Plains. The prairie sod was too tough for an ordinary plow to cut, and even the steel plow required three horses and little brother adding weight to do the job. If there was no drought, or ice storm, or plague of grasshoppers (which sometimes ate all the crop and even the plow handles), the rich soil produced a rich harvest. Some settlers of the West thought farming or ranching too chancy and relied on the pioneer's need for manufactured goods. But even businesses such as the peddler's wagon (83) or the optimistically named City Meat Market (84) demanded the whole family's efforts to succeed. The peddler's little boy and girl helped stock the drygoods wagon; the butcher's family stuffed sausages and waited on trade and considered themselves gentry because they lived in town and not in a sod hut on a land claim.*

85

86

Families had to pull together in pre-World War I America to make the family enterprise—farm or business—pay enough to support them. Then the women had to put in another day's worth of work in the house. (85) Many farmers left their wives in charge of the family accounts; and with mortgages, fluctuating crop prices, and animal diseases, it was dreary enough work. (86) These coal miners' wives living in Bethlehem, Pennsylvania, around 1906 were allowed to go down to the mine and glean dropped coal. If they didn't get enough, the family might freeze during the winter, since no miner could afford to buy the "black gold" he spent his energy dredging from the earth.   (87) For middle-class women in comfortable circumstances, like Mrs. Bernard of Long Island and her daughter, normal housekeeping in the first decade of the century was grinding and primitive work. To wash clothes, water had to be pumped up by hand and heated on a stove, and the dirt had to be rubbed out of the cloth against a scrubbing board. (88–90) In the immigrant ghettos of New York's Lower East Side, families worked together not to maintain family land or a business, but to obtain subsistence wages. Embroidery, "piece work," or cigar-making (twelve hours a day) brought in a few dollars a week.

88

89

90

Families who worked together in small trades or stores sometimes weathered the Depression. (92) The fruit stand of the significantly named Mr. Dollar was photographed in the 1920s when times were good. (91) In 1942 a "Ma and Pa" Italian restaurant in New York still flourished. (93) This fisherman who operates a boat off the coast of Maine is probably as confident that his son will follow his trade as is the tycoon-owner of a multimillion-dollar enterprise.

91

92

G.R. DOLLAR & SONS

93

Today, only the very poor, who have no options, and the very rich, who have no other options as good, work together as families. (94) Here a migrant laborer hoes Long Island potato fields with her children in 1951.

Most American families today work independently of each other. (95), Many women work outside the home, but others labor as the many-dutied chauffeur, cook, house-cleaner, and nurse that modern homemaking demands (96), Many men commute to a work area miles away from their homes, as these men did in the 1950s. Seldom is there any natural contact between work and family. Children growing up in this environment frequently do not choose their fathers' trades because they don't really know how their fathers spend their work time.

Proud Possessors

If you look at an old or modern photograph to see what you can discover you, may find clues that will tell you quite a lot about why people had their picture taken and what kind of people they were. Any activity can be photographed—working, playing, eating are all unmistakable when you see them—and the activity may well have been the reason for the photograph. What the activity demanded—a joint effort—or what it indicated about the subjects' lives—that they were happy together—may also have been sufficient reason for the picture. From the earliest days, one frequent motive in having a photograph taken was to record and immortalize something a family was proud of. Whether it was the biggest mansion in town, with a black coachman seated on the family rig out front; or a new roadster coupe and new raccoon coats; or an art collection that took two generations to assemble; or the fastest motorcycle made—whether it was these or a hundred other things, possessions were enough reason to get out the camera and record the moment.

Possessions have always had great importance in American life; they offered a means of asserting oneself as a civilized being in the vast wilderness and, later, of asserting one's superiority in a democracy based on personal achievement. Since the days of the Puritans, when material success indicated to your neighbors that you were in a state of grace and favor with God, *things* have made the man.

At first, pride in achievement was more common than pride in accumulation. Quilts and samplers worked by the women in a family, a bumper crop or a fine horse that a man raised were fit objects of pride. The spectacular vegetables that the Wisconsin pioneers displayed for the photographer in the picture on pages 120 and 121 were the result of a summer's drudgery and fears and battling with hailstorms and grasshoppers; equally important, they expressed the abundance the new land could give.

Yankee ingenuity slowly turned the economy after the Civil War from an agrarian to an industrial one. Industry and its riches became "property," instead of land. Mass production made more "things" available and, ironically, made them so similar that it took more of them to prove that the owner was different from —i.e., superior to—his neighbors. By the centennial year of 1876, mere possession had become more important than what was possessed. A decorating book of the time avowed, "Provided that there is room enough to move about without walking over the furniture, there is hardly likely to be too much in a room."

A full-scale flood of consumer goods in the twentieth century and the attendant snobbery about "brand names" gave Americans the chance to be very proud of their possessions indeed. Department stores, crammed to their unprecedentedly high tenth floors, flourished in America. Families in every city relied on Gump's or Marshall Field's or Horne's or Bloomingdale's or Macy's for everything from safety pins to haute couture. The most commonplace object was sanctified by a "good" name, and families appropriated brand names like armorial bearings: "We always used Gold Medal flour at home," "We always drove a Packard," or smoked Marsh Wheelings, or washed with Ivory Snow. Instead of identifying consumer goods according to the buyer's use, as had been done before the late nineteenth century—for instance, "a lady's shoe," "a baker's cap"—people began to identify things according to the *maker*. Americans have always felt that they were constructing a whole new civilization from scratch, and the uniformity of brand names seemed to carry assurance for people who otherwise had very few markers of civilization in common.

Trapped in consumerism now, we nonetheless remember the original miracle of abundance that America offered. It is still true that nothing is good in the United States unless it is big and there is a lot of it. The fact that this is no longer a young country (and, like old people, old countries become fat) has not dispelled our inherited belief in the importance of five or six chickens in every pot.

(97) *From being a rich man's toy in 1900, when there were only eight thousand of them, the automobile became the great symbol of achievement for every American. When it was photographed in 1915, this Thomas cost more than $3000. That stood for considerable achievement.*

(98) *Pride in American abundance was often justified by immense toil. Scandinavian emigrants to Wisconsin in 1895 were rightly proud of their array of gargantuan vegetables and of their baby's delicate christening robe—all homemade.* (99) *Jointly held possessions can build a family's sense of their importance as a social unit. Owning the biggest house in town, such as this one in a village near Boston around the turn of the century, with the appurtenances of a black yardman and a fine rig, was a sign of family prosperity as sure as money in the bank. There were no home-improvement loans or installment payments then.* (100) *The elegance of the twenties was epitomized by this Harlem couple, who hired photographer James Van Der Zee to record their Dusenberg auto and raccoon coats. In 1926 the car cost $7000 and the coats $300 each.*

101

(101, 102) *Different objects engender family pride in different social contexts, but the resulting satisfaction is much the same. The suburban California couple's delight in possessing gleaming motorcycles, a boat, and a car is not very different from the pride of the de Young sisters of San Francisco in the paintings their tycoon father collected and in the museum they built.*

(103) *Except for the native American—the Indian—this is how all our ancestors arrived. Everyone's first experience of this continent came at the end of a grueling move, but most immigrants came from families that had been tied to a small patch of European earth for centuries, and they regarded moving freely as a privilege.*

Mobility

Nothing in history is comparable to this continuous movement of mankind except perhaps that which followed the fall of the Roman Empire. Then as now, men in crowds converged on the same point, jostling together in the same places; but the designs of Providence were different then. Then each newcomer brought death and destruction in his train, but now it is the seed of life and of prosperity that he bears.   ALEXIS DE TOCQUEVILLE, *Democracy in America*, 1839

The uprootedness of the upper-middle class, I would say, almost parallels the uprootedness of migrant farm workers. In both cases, families tend to feel that they can't get too close to anything because they may be transferred—told to move on. And American business, it seems to me, trains its executives in a kind of aloofness that complements and helps sustain this mobility.
                    ROBERT COLES, interview, *Psychology Today*, November 1975

One hundred thirty-seven years ago, Alexis de Tocqueville, a small, dapper Frenchman fascinated by America, wandered through its lofty forests and red-brick villages making sharp-eyed observations; more recently, Robert Coles, a lanky Harvard professor and psychiatrist, sat in his basement office in Cambridge and talked about America. Both men remarked on the mobility, restlessness, adaptability—call it what you will—that is an outstanding characteristic of Americans. De Tocqueville saw it as life-bringing, Coles as "a kind of aloofness"—almost a denial of life. How did this shift in opinion come about?

For Americans, geographical mobility has always been identical with upward social and economic mobility. With a whole vast continent lying almost untouched for the first two hundred years of our history and then only slowly settled for the next hundred, a man and his family could, until seventy-five years ago, always move on when things weren't going well at home. Furthermore, when the railroads opened up the continent in the 1870s, economic ventures came to be twice as profitable when they were connected with movement. There were new markets and new ways of transporting goods to them. Texas beef was shipped to Chicago, slaughtered, and then refrigerated for shipment back to Texas and out to California and clear "down east" to Maine. The railroads that carried beef and steel and grain were themselves among the biggest money makers and most powerful industries in the nation, appropriating and controlling thousands of acres of new land. Therefore, in the first place because movement offered new land to Americans, and then because the vast spaces of the nation made transportation itself an economically sound enterprise, movement came to be viewed as a good thing. The Methodist Church for many years "rotated" its ministers, leaving them at the same church for only two years, so that they would be more objective, developing few community ties. For many management-level company employees today, a promotion automatically means moving the family to another city. Disdaining Benjamin Franklin's assertion that "a rolling stone gathers no moss," Americans have always rolled from coast to coast gathering and discarding moss of all sorts as they wandered.

From the outset we have been a migrant people. Except for the native Indians, everyone had to move here originally. And everyone came with hope, if not wild expectations. That trait of hoping for success over the next hill rather than just filling the shoes your father filled—or tilling the land your father tilled—has remained part of the American character. Potentially as good as anybody else, every American has thought that if he just *moved* into the right circumstances, he could prove it.

The wagon train was the first great means of conveyance—after the ship that brought them here in the first place. Wagons were used during the hundred years between 1790 and 1890, when the frontier was pushed from Ohio to Nevada. They were not usually the heavy Conestogas first used by Pennsylvania

127

teamsters but a plain board box about ten feet long, set directly on axles, with only a canvas covering to protect passengers from the rain, snow, and baking sun encountered on a three-month trek. Most wagons were pulled by a team of four or six oxen at the gruelingly slow rate of two miles per hour, which, in fact, preserved the bones of old people who would otherwise have been literally jolted to death. Moreover, children could get out and play and skip beside the wagon train that moved more slowly than a normal man's walk. The wagon trains usually started to roll as soon as the sun was up, before breakfast. There was a stop at midday, from ten o'clock until two or three, so that people could rest and eat. Then fires were extinguished and the train moved on, averaging about sixteen miles per day. Francis Parkman, the nineteenth-century author of *The California and Oregon Trail*, remarked on the impression of size and substantiality that a wagon train community presented. He encountered one

> at noon on the 14th of September [when] a very large Santa Fe caravan came up. The plain was covered with the long files of their white-topped wagons, the close black carriages in which the traders travel and sleep, large droves of animals and men on horseback and on foot. They all stopped on the meadow near us. Our diminutive cart and handful of men made but an insignificant figure by the side of their vast and bustling camp.

If the benefits of moving in the early days were better economic opportunities and an increased sense of community control over circumstances, one adverse effect, then as now, was that people felt uprooted and were always tantalized by the greener grass on the other side of the fence. Once the wagon-train passengers disbanded in the raw bustling little Western town or fort, each settler moved out on his own to his government land claim. He knew, after the trek, that by banding together people can solve problems and force their will on the minority, but no *particular* community commanded his emotional allegiance. Moreover, there was always the chance of a gold strike on another claim farther along; there was always the chance there might be more money in sheep-ranching than in pushing cattle. And there was no reason not to find out.

This is why Americans have always seemed restless to Europeans, always moving from farm to farm, from home to boardinghouse, and from seat to seat on the trains that were hurtling them across the countryside at unprecedented rates of speed. With no stable community to assure one of company, everybody was always looking for somebody to talk to. Privacy was so often an unasked-for corollary of moving that everyone seemed desperate to ensure that company was taken advantage of when there was some around. In the railroad cars, the desire for company and movement produced a constant hectic passage to and fro.

Given the means of moving quickly that steamboats and trains provided in mid-century, people rushed to get there first, wherever "there" was. During some steamboat races, boilers stoked beyond capacity blew up, and the bodies of sportsmen, slaves, and humble immigrants were scattered all over the churning Mississippi or the Ohio. But if its boiler held, the hottest boat got there first. Trains were built lightly to speed their turning wheels over lines laid down in a matter of weeks (the first line to reach a certain point where the government wanted connections made often received a monopoly on serving the entire area for a number of years). An English engine imported in 1829—the first to be used commercially in this country—was left to rust after a few trips because it was too heavy for the cheap bridge it had to cross. Getting the bridge across the creek in a hurry was more important than taking long enough to build a good one. The result of this mania for speed—and the fascination with it—was the risk of death or maiming in the course of the most routine journey. Statistics for train and steamboat accidents in the nineteenth century were regarded in the same way the statistics of automobile accidents are today. They were inevitable and appalling, but they deterred no one from traveling. After all, as a fellow train-passenger told Charles Dickens when he visited America in 1841, "Yankees are reckoned to be considerable of a go-ahead people."

Another result of the mania for speed and dependency on quickly erected and sometime inferior equipment was that Americans became very proficient—or "handy"—with machinery and made many technological advances. The most effective piece of technology created out of the desire for speed was seen for what it was by an old man in Muncie, Indiana, when interviewers asked him the principal difference between life when he was young and life in the 1920s. "Why on earth do you need to study what's changing this country? I can tell you what's happening in just four letters: A-U-T-O!"

Before the automobile became a common piece of domestic machinery, Americans' mobility consisted in moving their place of residence frequently, not moving just their bodies frequently. Until the 1920s, it was expensive to use trains or boats or horses as an amusement. The earlier American did not consider himself tied to an ancestral piece of land or trade guild, as people did in Europe. He could "pull up stakes" (an interesting metaphor since it originally described packing up the impermanent tent) and he could ship goods halfway across the country—thereby giving himself the option of living at a distance from his markets—but he didn't personally gad about.

Then came the car. Before there were cars, young couples courted in the parlor, millworkers lived within walking distance of the mill, everyone attended church twice on Sunday and one evening during the week, and people went to their lodges or visited neighbors for recreation. In 1910 there were 500,000 passenger cars in the United States, in 1918 there were 5,500,000, and by 1924—six years later—there were 15,500,000: a 3,000 percent increase in the number of automobiles in fourteen years.

At first, many families saw the car as a way of holding the family together against the onslaughts of the movies and telephone, both of which tended to fragment family life. One woman said, "I never feel as close to my family as when we are all in the car." But soon it was realized that, in fact, the car provided privacy and a means of escaping from the family. By the 1920s you weren't doing anything unless you went somewhere—in the car. Leisure had been remade and redefined, and with it family responsibilities and pleasures.

Before 1900 mobility in America was, quite literally, freedom. It offered the freedom to own land, the freedom to succeed, and the freedom to govern oneself. The work that this freedom demanded, in turn, strengthened family ties because the whole family had to hang together to achieve their freedom in the wilderness.

The automobile and the effects of the technological revolution in terms of industrial jobs appeared at the same time that the frontier disappeared. Mobility ceased to be an orderly progression of family units toward new land, becoming instead a hectic, almost pointless running back and forth in search of employment.

Today, migrant workers, people belonging to underprivileged ethnic minorities, follow the crops and harvests from south to north with the changing seasons and endure poverty as severe as that suffered by eighteenth- and nineteenth-century European peasants, without the security of those peasants' attachment to the land. In the migrants' case, mobility has only disadvantages. To the upper-middle-class executive who is transferred every year or two, mobility brings material advantages but no sense of personal control at all. His is the reverse of the early settlers' experience when they developed a government from community needs. Now, for the mobile executive, suburb succeeds suburb, each physically identical to the next. The families in each are as isolated from other families as are the figures in a dream who open their mouths and reach out their hands, but do not speak or touch.

In just the last few years there seems to be increasing resistance on the part of corporation employees to forced and frequent moving. A *New York Times* article of November 7, 1975, quoted an executive who had moved twelve times in eighteen years: "There comes a point in your life [when] a high rung on the corporate ladder isn't that important because sometimes you're losing more [in the move] than you're gaining." The wives of transferred executives have to start all over in each new town: make friends, find doctors and dentists, and often find new jobs, and their objections almost certainly have added to their husbands' doubts. In 1974 the Atlas Van Lines moving company reported that 57 percent of their client companies encountered refusals from employees who were to be transferred.

A symbol of where mobility has carried Americans might be the burgeoning trailer parks full of "mobile homes" that spread across America with chrome awnings and tiny garden plots. The trailer park is the opposite—a mirror image—of the covered wagon and what it stood for. The covered wagon was a poor shelter; life in it was replete with hardship, and it was very definitely only a temporary home until you got somewhere. Its advantages were that it provided travel with a community and that it offered a way to a new life. The mobile home is rarely mobile at all, it can only be transported behind a truck driven by a professional on certain roads for a limited distance. It is as full of conveniences as the covered wagon was of trouble and is intended to be a permanent residence. The mobility of the mobile home is putative, whereas that of the covered wagon was a fact. Mobile homes, despite their placement in a park, are intended to detach people from the responsibilities of yards, communities, and even families. Living in a mobile home is supposed to make you "carefree."

The lack of cares can also, however, be a lack of connections to anything worth caring about. As Americans seek to define their largest community—the nation itself—as it moves into its third century, they may find that the smaller communities of family and town provide many goals and rewards for those who settle and cultivate them.

105

106

(104) *During most of the nineteenth century, going West to new land meant an arduous wagon trip. The trek was made in the company of other families for safety's sake, and one modern historian surmises that the experience of deciding as a group what to do about such crises as Indian attacks, dying oxen, and snowstorms was a seedbed for American democracy. The birdcage in the wagon at right symbolizes the pioneers' determination to civilize as well as settle the West.* (105) *The nation's great waterways were corridors for the westward movement. A boat such as this one on the Missouri River might be loaded to the gunwales with people who had not slept in beds for more than a week.* (106) *When the transcontinental railroad finally stretched across the nation in 1869, transportation was easier and markets more accessible to farmers and ranchers on new land. For many country families, the railroad was the only contact with the world beyond the village. The romance of the railroad can be sensed in this photograph of families at the depot in Haines Corners, New York. Some of them may be "going abroad," as any trip of more than a few miles was described; or the little girls may simply have felt that a visit to the station required white dresses and parasol, usually kept for best.*

107

The automobile was the most revolutionary means of moving around to appear on the continent since the Indians got horses from the Spanish. It ultimately put speed and movement into family life and charged it with excitement, as this amateur auto race in Pennsylvania's Pocono Mountains suggests (107). (109) In the depths of the Depression of the 1930s, Oklahoma farmers—the earth blown off their fields by relentless winds—made the same migration West in old Fords that their ancestors had made in covered wagons seventy-five years earlier. The trip was quicker, but there were no rewards when they arrived; all the land was gone. (108) Modern families, such as this one in the 1950s, could pack up and spend a weekend together—or they could split up and travel separately with ease.

109

108

(110) *The weekend camper has replaced the covered wagon as a home on wheels.*
(111) *The six million people living in trailer parks in this country aren't actually mobile; their homes are meant to be hauled by truck for short distances only. But neither are they settled. They claim the privileges of mobility and pay no taxes; they have few connections with any community beyond the gates of their parks.*

Being Parents

Louisa May Alcott was the most popular children's writer of her day. From their first appearance in the 1870s, her "little men" and "little women" seemed unusually plucky, straightforward, and real to children who were accustomed to seeing themselves depicted in the morally improving McGuffey's Readers of the time as dim, milky allegories of Right and Wrong. Miss Alcott's children, although unwearyingly guided toward the graceful state of Christian gentility, got tired, bored, and rebellious, and sometimes even were right. When they were right, it meant, of course, that their preceptors were wrong—as in the case of Billy Ward in *Little Men.* Billy

> was what the Scotch tenderly call an "innocent." He had been an unusually intelligent boy, and his father had hurried him on too fast, giving him all sorts of hard lessons, keeping him at his books six hours a day, and expecting him to absorb knowledge as a Strasbourg goose does the food crammed down its throat. He thought he was doing his duty, but he nearly killed the boy, for a fever gave the poor child a sad holiday, and when he recovered, the overtasked brain gave out, and Billy's mind was like a slate over which a sponge has passed, leaving it blank. It was a terrible lesson to his ambitious father.

The notion of the child as the overstuffed Strasbourg goose who will one day produce pâté de fois gras was a brilliant stroke on the part of Miss Alcott, for it reflected a basic American attitude toward children: They are raw material whose forming is a reflection of the parents' own skill. Generations of American schoolchildren have wondered if they were being pushed into a dilemma such as Billy's and hoped, if so, that their parents would be sorry.

The concept of childhood as a separate state of mind and development did not gain general acceptance before the eighteenth century. Until then, the medieval notion that humanity was divided into helpless infants and adults—albeit some smaller than others—was generally held. Medieval children were put to work at six or seven years of age in the fields, betrothed at nine or ten, and married at the onset of puberty. They were dressed like little adults (even to miniature suits of armor for pint-sized aristocrats), and they were expected to display the judgment and moral discrimination of adults (in some seventeenth-century American colonies it was a hanging crime for a child over sixteen years of age to strike a parent). Because of this view, seventeenth-century—and particularly Puritan—notions of child-rearing were strict. If children were limited adults, then they had the moral and religious responsibilities of adults, and the essential responsibility of a Puritan adult was to demonstrate that he was living in a state of grace. The signs of grace tended to coincide with the outward signs of decorum and prosperity. Now, children have no means of demonstrating prosperity on their own, and in the thousands of years of recorded history they have never been notable for a sense of decorum. The one means of demonstrating that a Puritan child was at least not damned outright was the fact of baptism. Many fragile little bundles were sent almost direct to heaven by being taken out to church for baptism in the blustery New England winter. After the child's baptism, the Puritan parent was faced quite literally with whipping it into line so it would demonstrate adult virtues. There was only one standard for everybody; transgression was transgression whether you were six and rolled a hoop on the Sabbath or were thirty-six and begot a bastard on your neighbor's widow. The duty of a seventeenth-century parent was to curb the tendency to original sin. If a parent spared the rod, he was likely to be reprimanded by the community for the sin of indulgence himself.

(112) *Being a parent is the most demanding permanent job that exists. In New York City slums in the 1890s, when social reformer Jacob Riis made this rare kinetic photograph of a mother rushing to her children, the hazards of disease and lack of food compounded more ordinary dangers.*

And then, during the eighteenth century, everything slowly began to change. In France, Jean-Jacques Rousseau propounded the optimistic theory that man was basically good, not basically evil, and, as the theories of Sigmund Freud were to do a century and a quarter later, Rousseau's writings percolated down from the intellectual elite to become the common intellectual baggage even of people who disagreed with him. The broad social and economic opportunities of the New World played an important role in furthering the shift in attitude. Because children could strike out on their own soon after entering adolescence, they became especially valuable to parents who needed their labor and were afraid of losing them. At the same time, these social and economic forces were encouraging Americans generally on a liberal course that would eventually cause them to call all men equal and declare themselves independent of Mother England.

Even before Rousseau's influence had become effective, the tight Puritan community was diffusing into a complex, seafaring merchant society, and the alternatives for adults were multiplying. Children had to be prepared to face a multitude of opportunities. So instead of little vessels of original sin who had to be judged on adult terms, children began to be seen as blank slates on which the parents were responsible for writing worthwhile messages. Education, rather than constraint, became the primary parental concern.

After the breakdown of the colonial social system in which everyone had been subordinate to the community interest, the family unit became largely independent. Oriented toward the future, the family inevitably underwent a shift in internal focus, and children were given tacit, and sometimes explicit, first place in their parents' lives. The schools reflected the attitude of the doting parents who worshipped their children at home, and, despite the fact that public education was highly valued in America—and as widely disseminated as in the more sophisticated countries (by 1850, 50 percent of the adult American population was literate)—discipline was always something of a problem.

One of the favorite bits of American frontier folklore concerns the new teacher who would be beaten up by the "big boys"—often his contemporaries—unless he could beat them up first with his fists or a blacksnake whip. A man who grew up in western Pennsylvania in the first decade of the century remembers a woman who taught at his one-room school wrestling a refractory eighth-grader to the floor and sitting on him the rest of the day while she taught. Discipline in the schools had only limited effect because the children lived at home, and the schools only existed by consent of the parents sitting on school boards.

Despite its late entry into human history, the new concept of childhood as a unique stage of life developed rapidly in the early nineteenth century. Segregating children in schools away from adults helped to emphasize their separate state and, for the first time, books were written especially for children. The first American edition of *Mother Goose* appeared in Boston in 1833, about the time that the first two American children's books, *Tales of Peter Parley About America* and *Little Rollo* came out (in 1827 and 1834, respectively). The newly perceived child was something of a literary concept, generally, and countless enthusiastic outpourings from adult pens helped forge the new creature. Van Wyck Brooks, New England's literary historian, has said that "children filled the scene. All the New England writers understood them and wrote about them, sometimes with exquisite feeling. . . . Hawthorne's stories were as full of children as ever the summer woods were filled with birds; and Whittier's shy affections and Holmes's salty humours were addressed as often as not to boys and girls." Even Mr. Emerson wrote about children in his essay "Domestic Life." As an example of the nineteenth-century writers' sensitivity to children, Brooks quotes a passage from a Harriet Beecher Stowe story: "Pliable as she was to all outward appearance, the child had her own still, interior world, where all her little notions and opinions stood up crisp and fresh, like flowers that grow in cool, shady places. If anybody assailed a thought or suggestion she put forth, she drew it back again into this quiet inner chamber and went on. . . . there is no independence and pertinacity like that of these seemingly soft, quiet creatures, whom it is so easy to silence, and so difficult to convince." The innocence of nature had replaced Divine Grace as the ruling moral force.

These cherished and carefully cultivated children were treated as adults in nineteenth-century America as they had been earlier, but in a very different way, for the Puritans had imposed adult moral responsibilities on them, whereas the nineteenth century gave them adult freedom. And to this the ubiquitous British travelers took strong exception. In 1867 one of these, Greville Chester, called American children "small stuck-up caricatures of men and women, with but little of the fresh ingenuousness and playfulness of childhood." In 1875 Therese Yelverton remarked, "A child with rosy cheeks and bright joyous laugh, its docile obedience and simplicity, its healthful play and its disciplined work, is a being almost unknown in

America." (One questions whether the being thus described was ever known anywhere.) But there was another side to the picture. Nineteenth-century American parents did not feel that their children had to be whipped into submission and left as subjects for a Dickens novel in order to make them into human beings. Yet another traveler, after describing a man and his son, who were singing to each other to pass the time on a train, remarked wonderingly, "In America the father never loses sight of his child, who thus grows up as his companion and is soon . . . in some sort an equal."

American children's independence of will, we must note, was never meant to degenerate into sheer wilfulness. The wilderness was tamed not by whim but by effort. Sturdy little republicans who got their own ways were looked on fondly only as long as those ways followed some definite direction, and children were early set to doing useful tasks—girls sewing samplers, boys chopping wood or, later, delivering papers. Lydia Maria Child, who wrote a book in 1829 on what we would call home economics, intoned that it was better "for boys and girls to be picking blackberries at six cents a quart than to be wearing out their clothes in useless play." The emphasis on achievement, however, had a consequence undreamed of before the nineteenth century. Children who strove to outstrip each other chopping wood and picking berries might someday outstrip their parents. Equality in America was understood as equality of *opportunity*, and the opportunity was to rise above the station of one's birth. Margaret Mead wrote in 1942: "By and large, the American father has an attitude towards his children which may be loosely classified as autumnal. They are his for a brief and passing season, and in a very short while they will be operating gadgets which he does not understand and cockily talking a language to which he has no clue." So these American children who were given their heads and encouraged to pursue their interests to the limit of their strength, children who were treated as the equals of adults when they were small, grew up to be more than equals—in fact, to be their superiors. The best example of this often repeated occurrence in American life comes from the immigrant experience. The children in the newly arrived family learn English, play baseball, shorten their skirts, and undertake the education of their parents in the folkways of the new land. A late nineteenth-century photograph of an Italian boy sitting at a table with his father, who clenches a pipe tightly in his teeth in the desperate effort to understand the reading lesson his son is giving him, is a fine illustration of the bittersweet nature of the process. For Americans who had been here longer than one generation, the process was more subtle but just as paradoxical.

Their children's progress, viewed emotionally, was regrettable and often left parents with feelings of desertion and even resentment. Viewed rationally, it was just what they had hoped for and intended. It was, in fact, the justification of their efforts. They had been responsible for creating successful, independent beings. In *Portnoy's Complaint*, Philip Roth's recent novel of cultures in collision, Alexander Portnoy asks his omnipresent psychiatrist, "What *was* it with these Jewish parents, *what*, that they were able to make us little Jewish boys believe ourselves to be princes on the one hand, unique as unicorns on the one hand, geniuses and brilliant like nobody has ever been brilliant and beautiful before in the history of childhood—saviors and sheer perfection on the one hand and such bumbling, incompetent, thoughtless, helpless, selfish, evil little . . . *ingrates,* on the other!" It was in America, the land of promise, with no past and all the future that these conflicts flowered and bloomed. To emigrant parents from the *shtetl,* the ghetto, the Sicilian village baking in the sun, and even to poor families in the old settled cities of the Eastern seaboard, for two hundred years opportunity beckoned, and parents like Louisa May Alcott's fictional Mr. Ward and Alexander Portnoy's mother stuffed their children like Strasbourg geese with the goods and chances of the New World.

The shift in the perception of children from small creatures of sin who must be disciplined to bits of the future who must be cherished occurred approximately one hundred years before another radical change in child-rearing. In the 1920s, with the development of penicillin and other modern drugs, the physical care of children became a much less precarious undertaking than it had been. Human children require physical care and nurture longer than the young of any other animal species; and, until after World War I, one child out of five in America did not survive its first two years. Disease was rampant, and, in fact, the raw milk substituted for that of a mother who was unable to nurse her child probably had as much disease as nourishment in it. Historians theorize that seventeenth- and eighteenth-century American parents treated their babies the way animals treat their offspring: They were cared for with great zeal but if they died they were forgotten without much mourning. A generalization such as this does not take the range of individual emotional reactions into account, of course, but it can reflect a widespread attitude. In America's first three hundred years, children

141

could be so easily snatched away by the mysteries of sickness and death that their parents could not count on any one child's survival; and, because of this, children were taken for granted as part of the natural cycle of the years—the planting, harvesting, changes of seasons, and birth and death of animals.

For the frontier parent, the act of survival naturally included childbirth just as it naturally included work: Both were necessities. The value of children in the aggregate precluded emphasizing the importance of any one child. By the 1920s, however, technology and industry had provided more opportunities for adults as well as better care for children. Food, shelter, and clothing could be obtained by the efforts of fewer family members, and the loss of a job usually did not carry the threat of starvation as the loss of a crop often did in the old days; the basic relationships of society, such as those between spouses and between parents and children, came about because of arbitrary decisions rather than by necessity. For instance, a woman no longer had to marry in order to provide a home for herself; instead she could take a job. Similarly, people did not have to have children to help them in their work. Financially, in fact, children were an economic luxury rather than a help. The family's economic need for children lessened at the same time that every child's health and life were practically assured by the new drugs. Children often became status symbols and could provide a reason for existing in a world that had lost its old simplicities. The modern parent in Anne Richardson Roiphe's novel *Up the Sandbox* feels this way about her baby son and daughter: "I am almost his possession. Elizabeth's too. My selfish purposes are also served, as the children make for me a universe, with a design and a rhythm and a function. And instead of being, as I was before I conceived a child, a bit of dark matter orbiting aimlessly, brooding on my own molecular disintegration, I am now a proper part of ordinary society." No nineteenth-century parent needed children to make them feel "a proper part of ordinary society"; the mere struggle for day-to-day subsistence made them that.

With children more of a luxury and less of an unquestioned presence in social and economic life, it is less and less clear how you should shape your child. Many people no longer think they have to save him from sin, nor do they have to train him for the family business. Now, with women looking outside the home for interests and men still engaged in the rat-race of a competitive, industrialized society, the possibility exists that you won't shape your child at all. As long ago as 1925, a father in *Middletown* said, "I'm a rotten dad. . . . If our children amount to anything it's their mother who'll get all the credit. I'm so busy I don't see much of them and I don't know how to chum up with them when I do." No seventeenth- or eighteenth- or nineteenth-century father whose son's help was essential for the family worried about "chumming up" with him. Forty-five years after *Middletown* was written, Anne Roiphe worried that "the baby must have what the books call consistent mothering or his small soul will warp and bend in strange directions, and he might decide it's not worth growing and reverse the process, curl himself in fetal position and look only inward, refusing food until life itself is extinguished. . . . I make life again each day like Penelope weaving a shroud never to be completed until Ulysses returns." "Consistent mothering" was the daily reality for a frontier woman whose life, in fact, resembled that of Penelope's, over three thousand years before, in its diurnal routine of weaving, brewing, baking, and nursing. The mere fact that a modern mother can objectify the process of mothering and worry about its outcome shows how far we have come from the natural nurturing of earlier years.

But finally, whatever function parents see their children as performing, for most children the parents are the consistent and stable fact of their world. The little Puritan child in adult britches or cap, switching home the cows; the pioneer child running beside the covered wagon as it trundled heavily along the trail; the only child of the 1920s who graduated from bottle to playpen; the 1970s baby who moves from its mother's breast to creative playthings—the feelings of all are expressed in the litany James Agee ascribes to a small child:

> I hear my father; I need never fear.
> I hear my mother; I shall never be lonely, or want for love.
> When I am hungry it is they who provide for me; when I am in dismay, it is they who fill me with comfort.
> When I am astonished or bewildered, it is they who make the weak ground firm beneath my soul: it is in them that I put my trust.

Providing this stability is and has always been the first function of parenting.

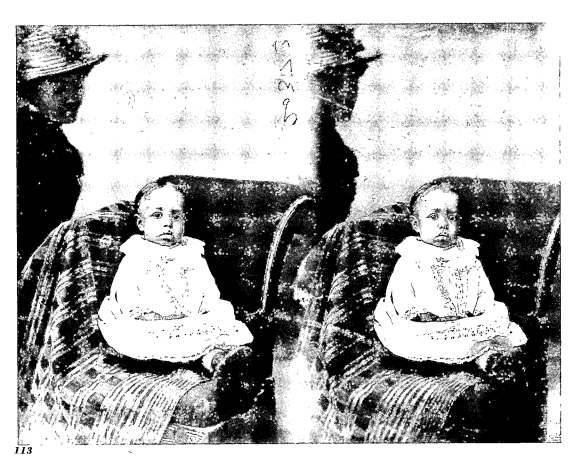

(113) *The always watchful vigilance of a mother is suggested by this photograph taken in Cooperstown, New York, in 1885 of Kate Taylor, a black seamstress and her baby daughter.* (114) *This sod farmer of Custer Country, Nebraska, was a widower with three small children. The waterlogged roof of his sod house collapsed just before the photographer arrived, but, despite living in a mud house and farming ten hours a day, the farmer had a clean white dress for his little girl.*

113

114

(115) *Bringing up children in poverty circumstances means fighting symptoms—such as lice—without being able to eliminate causes—such as dirt. "Cracking lice" was a parental duty for poor Americans, black and white alike, for decades. Few threats to children are permanently eradicated; in 1976 there was an epidemic of lice in a school in a middle-class neighborhood in Brooklyn, New York. (116) Children's manners as well as their physical beings need attention. For an upper-middle-class family in 1911, having tea together was an important experience: This girl will have to serve tea some day; the boys may court their future wives in such surroundings. (117) Minding their manners when shopping with Mother has always been a grim job for young men, whether in New York City in 1914 or today.*

115

116

117

The rewards and burdens of parenthood are both experienced as soon as the child is born. (118) The pleasant though serious business of rearing a child in the prosperous 1920s is suggested by this tranquil view of a father, mother, and baby (with a fashionable Dutch-bob haircut) spending the afternoon at Lake Otsego, New York. (119) The hard job of feeding a family was very much on the minds of young Americans like this Ohio couple, who were caught in the middle of the Great Depression in 1934. The photograph suggests that their baby was more of a faceless burden than a person to them in that time of stress. (120) In wartime, a mother is often left to cope with children alone. In 1942 one mother paused in New York's Pennsylvania Station to adjust her baby's coverlet.

118

119

120

121

122

123

(121) *When both children want the family bike, it takes mother's arbitrating hand to make it clear that if one brother has the swing, the other deserves to cycle for a while.* (122) *The conflicts between house rules and a young personality's need to assert itself can bring storms such as this one in Connecticut. The disemboweled Santa Claus is evidence that destruction of property does not go unpunished on this domestic front.* (123) *Parents often feel their children's hurts and triumphs more deeply than the child himself. This blue-ribboned winner of a Texas rodeo contest seems less concerned about his further chances of success than does his mother.*

125

Urging new goals, solving problems, and just plain being there at all times makes a parent's job seem roughly equivalent to managing a small corporation. (124) The urgent need for toilet-training and the possibility of reverberations throughout the child's life if the process is mishandled—according to modern psychologists—demand from parents an approach delicately balanced between coercion and encouragement. (125) Mother as the all-powerful fixer who makes everything right exists for children until they are adolescents and face conflicts that are beyond their parents' ability to solve. (126) The parent becomes an island of security in a big, alien world, particularly when a small child feels lost at knee-level in a crowd of adults. This boy tenderly examined the always-familiar, always-shifting map of love in his father's face when they both attended a Civil Rights demonstration at the Lincoln Memorial in the early 1960s.

Play

Humanity seems determined to make fun of itself. For every bland, virtuous hero and heroine of *Love's Labours' Lost* or *The Magic Flute,* there has to be a wisecracking, snapping, sparring Beatrice and Benedick or a capering Papageno and Papagena, done up in ridiculous bird's feathers. For every brave, thick-muscled Brom van Bones, the suitor of Katrina van Tassel in "The Legend of Sleepy Hollow," there has to be an innocent and gawky Ichabod Crane. For every Tom Sawyer, all sticky sweet on Becky Thatcher, there has to be a Huck Finn, determined to light out for the territories at the first sight of a civilized curl or pantalette. And we, the readers or viewers of books, plays, TV, and life itself are caught in a dilemma. The perfect heroes we all know—the man whose car never stalls on a snowy morning or the Little Leaguer who always hits a home run—are certainly admirable and necessary to remind us all that perfection exists. But we don't really like them. It's Papageno and Beatrice and Ichabod and Huck that we like; they're the ones we remember.

It's now a psychological commonplace that jokes are a means of dealing with real issues, and games are often training grounds and arenas for competition. The reason we like comic characters is because we feel close to them; they represent things that bother us—awkwardness around the other sex, squandering money, being a victim of big business—without making us deal directly with those worries. When children, adolescents, or adults laugh or play, they're in touch with their deeper feelings and concerns without being threatened by them. Play is being able to knock father's croquet ball into the middle of next week without openly declaring we hate father because he wouldn't let us have the car Friday night. Play is especially vital in a child's life because it helps him learn about relationships in his world, learn adult roles, and learn about himself. For adults as well as children, play is said to resemble dreams in function: Both play and dreams provide crazy, jumbled images of the "real" world that replay and anticipate its stresses and challenges. In both play and dreams, you can practice or get another chance.

In America today, we play a lot of games, both in formal, structured situations and informally. This wasn't always the case. Seventy-five years ago, play was mostly informal—neighborhood pick-up baseball rather than Little League. Three hundred years ago there was hardly any play acknowledged as such, at all.

Those earnest moralists the Puritans thought that idleness—which was synonymous with games and play—was sinful. Anyhow, nobody had time for it if the colony was to stave off the Indians and the Devil, both lurking on the fringes of the forest to snatch the unwary idler, rolling his hoop along the path. Only unremitting "industrie" would keep the "city set upon a hill" in a state of grace and solvency. In 1630 the Puritans chased back to England the neighboring settlers of Merry-Mount, non-Puritans who had set up a maypole and danced "aboute it many days togeather, inviting the Indean women, for their consorts, dancing and frisking togither, (like so many fairies, or furies rather), and worse practises." But the Puritans with their notions of communal responsibility did set up one form of enduring play. It was effective as play is for small children in that it helped socialize people. At these working games everyone got together to raise a barn or build a wall or stitch a quilt. These "bees" turned work into play, anticipating Tom Sawyer, who got his friends to whitewash the fence for him, by two hundred years. If it was drudgery to build your own stone wall, it was your bounden duty to talk and drink and feast and build your neighbor's wall. It was play because you were not obliged, other than charitably, to make that wall, and it was the only kind of play those grim people recognized. Little New England maidens occasionally had wooden dolls known as

(127) *At Oak Bluffs, the Methodist campground and summer resort on Martha's Vineyard, in 1871, croquet was one of the few diversions the serious lecture-goers permitted themselves. Of course, it was all right to knock your opponent's ball halfway to heaven.*

"poppets," and the boys might have tops, but they had to be used circumspectly when the child's daily tasks were finished—and that might not be until dusk or bedtime.

One colony in the North that did not issue strictures against play that was not productive and mirth that did not directly glorify God was New Amsterdam, later known as New York. William Bradford of Massachusetts recorded that the Pilgrims left their earlier sanctuary in Holland for New England because of the "great licentiousness of youth" there, which they were afraid would corrupt their own small fry. The licentious Dutch brought skates and bowling on the green and sledding, not to mention the toy-laden Sint Klaas with them to the New World. Until the end of the eighteenth century, young people in New Amsterdam went around together in "companies," social clubs for both sexes and all ages from children to young adults. There were rival games and contests and parties between the companies, and a great deal of merrymaking.

The companies reflected the adult world as play almost always does. In New England, the only play was structured around work, because that was what the adult community emphasized. In the South, boys were taken hunting and riding because prowess and genteel accomplishments were important there. Girls in the South were given toy mirrors and dolls from London, tricked out in the latest styles for ladies to copy. New Amsterdam's children played in "companies" because the Dutch were a commercial people who lived by trade, and whose government in the New World was responsible not to the Estates-General of Holland but to the Dutch West India Company, which sponsored the colony in return for furs and raw material.

New Amsterdam parents were exceptional in the early days not only in granting such license to their children but also in encouraging them to develop a high degree of organization in the companies. "Structured" play would not appear again in the United States until the school-centered activities of the twentieth century. For most of the nineteenth century, children's play and family play fell into two categories. First, there continued to be work got up in the guise of play. As frontier settlements continued to spread across the nation, hard labor was often essential for survival. If neighbors could be found to help raise a log wall or "skutch" flax (beat the stalks to break down the fibers), then the purposes of both efficiency and pleasant socializing were served, but efficiency was the critical factor.

The other kind of play that youngsters engaged in during the nineteenth and early twentieth centuries was what was called "making their own fun." It has always been a hallowed myth that every American is an independent individual who can stand on his own two feet; American children, consequently, were supposed to explore their world and amuse themselves without help from anybody. There was still sufficient distrust of pure amusement, in any case, to make youthful play something that happened under society's nose, not with its cooperation; organized play with paid supervisors would have been unthinkable then, putting the stamp of approval on tomfoolery and idleness. The charm of idleness in a small town, with its opportunities for mischief and imagination (especially for boys), was extolled by Mark Twain and Booth Tarkington and remembered nostalgically by generations of adults. The reality of those hours, punctuated only by chores and church, was perhaps more deadly monotonous than sentimental adults remembered, and, as the country became more industrialized and faster moving, the possibilities of unstructured fun became more limited, with no alternative replacing it. Frederick Lewis Allen, American historian and sociologist, was writing about life at the turn of the century when he said:

> Consider, for example, what a small Midwestern town had to offer a boy by way of recreation and educational opportunity. Tradition said that boys must find their own chances for recreation— swimming at the old swimming hole of hallowed legend, playing baseball in the open fields, hunting and fishing in the neighboring woods and streams. But already industrialism was contaminating the rivers, the open country was being built up and cultivated, the natural playgrounds were being despoiled—and few substitute diversions had been provided.

Allen goes on to quote Clyde Brion Davis's memories of Chillicothe, Missouri:

> [There was no place] where a youngster could enter the water except the really filthy ponds and the equally dirty and dangerous river where drownings occurred every season. . . . We, in our district, had no place to play baseball except a wholly inadequate and rutty lot down by the Milwaukee

tracks. . . . There was no tennis or golf or badminton or basketball. There was not a gymnasium in town or anything approaching physical education even in high school.

On the other hand, because children were dependent on their own resources for play in the nineteenth century, there was much more family cooperation—in an informal sense. There were no clubs or organized games or school activities to go to, so a child's friends were likely to be the children of his parents' friends, and often play was just staying at home pulling taffy or singing around the parlor organ. Children's play seventy-five years ago was more likely to involve—and affect—the other family members than it is today. The author's father remembers playing a game with his brother that involved chasing each other through the rooms of the family farmhouse; at one point, afraid his brother would catch him, one of the boys tied one end of a string to a doorknob and the other end to a high narrow cupboard containing all the jellies and preserves "put up" for the winter. When the older brother pulled the door, he pulled the cupboard over. The smaller brother lit out for the cornfield, where he remained hidden until dinnertime, but the family never disciplined him because they were so glad to see him. They had been unable to lift the heavy cupboard, and the red jelly oozing out from under it could have been raspberries or it could have been little brother. The punishment, in any case, was the entire family's because a summer's preserving was wasted and there was no jelly for anybody all that long winter. He also remembers that for his people, Christmas and the church strawberry festival were the high points of the year. Such community affairs as the strawberry festival and Fourth-of-July parades heightened family fun. Children at home jumped into haymows from the barn rafters rather than a swimming pool from a diving board, as they do today. Excursions on interurban trolleys that ran through fields and along river banks were a favorite family diversion, just as automobile drives were when cars first became available (giving rise to the derogatory phrase "Sunday driver").

Haymows and trolleys were natural features of the landscape that could be used for fun. They were not constructed for the purpose of entertainment, unlike today's swimming pools and golf courses. The thin edge of that particular wedge entered the scene with the rise of the great American sport of baseball after the Civil War. Invented by a group of New York clubmen in the 1840s, baseball quickly spread among the workers of the cities and inhabitants of small towns. In 1869 the Cincinnati Red Stockings toured as the first professional athletic team the country had ever had, and the National League of Professional Baseball Clubs was established in 1876. But the immediate impact of baseball came not through the professional clubs, but through the amateur or "semi-pro" ball clubs that every town organized. Now there was something for young men—and even middle-aged men—to do besides sit on the front porch and work in the garden. Women and children came to watch the games, but their presence was incidental to the players' excitement. Fun now lay outside the family.

Baseball clubs were just the start of an avalanche of organizations and fads that took people out of their homes. Bicycles were the rage in the 1890s, requiring for the first time a large cash outlay for a frivolous item. The cash outlay didn't stop people, and 10 million Americans (out of a population of 70 million in 1900) rode bicycles. Fraternal organizations for men with their "women's auxiliaries" burgeoned, and in 1910, when William Boyce adapted the new English notion of boys' clubs, called the Boy Guides, into the Boy Scouts of America, everybody had a club. By the 1920s inhabitants of Indiana's "Middletown" scarcely saw their sons and daughters, except at the dinner table—sometimes. "Agencies drawing the child away from home multiply. Athletics, dramatics, committee meetings after school hours demand his support; YMCA, YWCA, Boy Scouts, Girl Reserves, the movies, auto-riding—all neighborhood concerns unknown to his parents in their youth—are centers of interest; club meetings, parties or dances, often held in public buildings, compete for his every evening."

Some Middletown parents in 1925 tried to keep up with their children in the new opportunities for play and fun family affairs, almost by brute force. One woman said: "I just can't afford to grow old. . . . I have a boy of fifteen in high school and another of thirteen. I put on roller skates with the boys and pass a football with them. In the evenings we play cards and on Sundays we go to ball games. My mother back East thinks its scandalous, but I tell her I don't think anything very bad can happen to boys when they're with their father and mother." But the very nature of the activities split up the family and gave more importance to one member than another; the whole family might go to watch the son play football at the high school several years after his mother tossed the ball around with him in the backyard, but the big game made the son a hero in a way that had little or nothing to do with that preparation at home. When parents weren't pursuing their own diversions (one Middletown girl said she hated the country club "because Mother is out there all the time"), they tried to join and assist their children in theirs. Yet another Middletown parent confessed, "I accommodate my entire life to my little girl. She takes three music lessons a week and I practice with her forty minutes a day. I help her with her school work and go to dancing school with her."

There was no stemming the tide, however, and sophisticated *social*—rather than familial or communal—activities took the place of the old diversions. Dancing and card playing were avowed to be Middletown's most popular leisure activities, and these were supplemented by the radio, the movies, and the automobile. Radio had some status as a means for disseminating news, and the automobile very quickly assumed a place in people's work lives, but all of these new machines had important functions as leisure-time fillers. The contrast between nineteenth-century options for play and amusement and twentieth-century ones comes across strongly in an 1892 ordinance passed in Indiana. "Any person convicted of having, on Sunday, within said city, pitched quoits, or coins, or of having played at cricket, bandy, cat, townball, or any other game of public amusement, or of having discharged any gun, pistol, or other firearms, shall be fined therefor in any sum not less than one dollar nor more than five dollars." Thirty years later the notion of blue laws against games was ludicrous, and they would have been hooted out of any town in America—for thirty years later people did not stay at home with their families on Sunday, still (in the 1920s) many wage earners' only leisure day. The very games outlawed in the 1890s on the Sabbath were usually informal and would have been played with family and neighbors. "Public amusement" was only relatively public then. There were no movie-theater chains backed by corporate financing; no radio stations disseminating popular tunes (and no records to play at public dances); and no cars to get women to bridge clubs across town, men to lodge meetings, and young people to basketball games twenty miles away. In the 1890s people were legally (if tacitly) encouraged to stay at home; by the 1920s they were induced with all the cunning international commerce could command to go out—separately.

Since the 1920s, organized play for both adults and children has almost completely routed casual play from the field. Although there are some family board games such as Monopoly and Clue, during leisure hours children and adults are more likely to be in separate rooms of the house enjoying spectator sports of some variety. The adult who, in 1900, played neighborhood baseball or "pitched quoits," now watches pro football on television. The child who built a tree house now can go to a Walt Disney movie. The children's-toy industry, producing talking, fighting G.I. Joe dolls and self-driving trucks, is the multimillion-dollar heir of the old craft shops that produced stiff wax dolls and Erector sets, which required a good deal of imagination from the child who played with them. And, of course, the television set, the all-pervasive assassin of spontaneous, imaginative play or leisure, spreads talking pictures of Captain Kangaroo, Star Trek, and Gunsmoke across the land.

From legislating, or at least discouraging, play out of existence, we have come around to mechanizing it away. Organization and technology have done their best to make play a matter of competition and pressing buttons, rather than an imaginative way of coming to terms with the "serious" world. But still . . . there is that little girl who lets several new dolls of glorious, lifelike complexion and abilities lie untouched while she hugs her old, eyeless yarn doll. A cliche? Yes, but the imagination is harder to quash than man periodically thinks. When the Puritans tried it, their imagination played tricks on them and they saw witches. When the child—or adult—has more toys than he can handle, he still is likely to weave fantasies around an old one and let the others go. And the fantasies will deal with that other hard world where the enemies of play come from. The only real threat to fantasy is not having enough time. We can organize play however we like. It won't make it much more or less significant. We can split families up while they're playing—children will still devote a lot of playtime to what they see in their families when they do see them. But if there is no time for play—then we'll be in trouble.

(128) *The Dakins were well-to-do upstate New Yorkers who had a summer house at Cherry Valley. One son was a photographer, who used a primitive gunpowder attachment (the flash is reflected in the mirror) to capture his family in gales of laughter, listening to a funny story told by Grandfather, at right in the white suit. This rare indoor photograph is unusual for its time (the 1880s) in its spontaneity, but families entertaining themselves was a common scene in the majority of households across the country.*

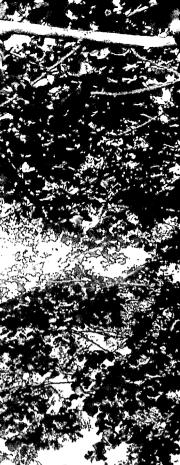

(129) *A three-generation camping trip such as this Oregon family took in 1915 required a welter of tin plates, coffee pots, and rustic benches to make everybody comfortable.* (130) *Climbing a tree in your best bib and tucker after Sunday dinner was equally exciting for this uncle and nephew, in a photograph taken in Wisconsin in the 1890s.* (131) *An Oregon camping trip could include a fish-spearing expedition when an old-timer took father and son to look for fresh salmon in a clear stream.*

132

133

Older people today say that winters used to be colder and snowier than they are now. (132) *In 1898 there was enough snow in Central Park for this boy to try hitching his dog to the family sled to give his sister a ride.* (133) *Snowball fights were a family affair on Long Island in 1905. Judging from the snow on his coat, Father seems to have gotten the worst of it.* (134) *As late as the 1920s, sitting on the beach required almost as many clothes as playing in the snow did.*

(135) *Flowers in an open field offered as much room for the imagination at the turn of the century as they do today.* (136) *In Washington, North Carolina, in 1938, when the farm family came to town on Saturday, there were provisions to be bought and perhaps the bank and the drugstore to visit, but the whole trip assumed the air of an excursion when Daddy treated everyone to ice-cream cones.* (137) *Morrisville, Vermont, had an annual fair, and one family camped on the fairgrounds for a week in the summer of 1936; the children enjoyed the wonderful week-long opportunity to play house in the car.*

136

137

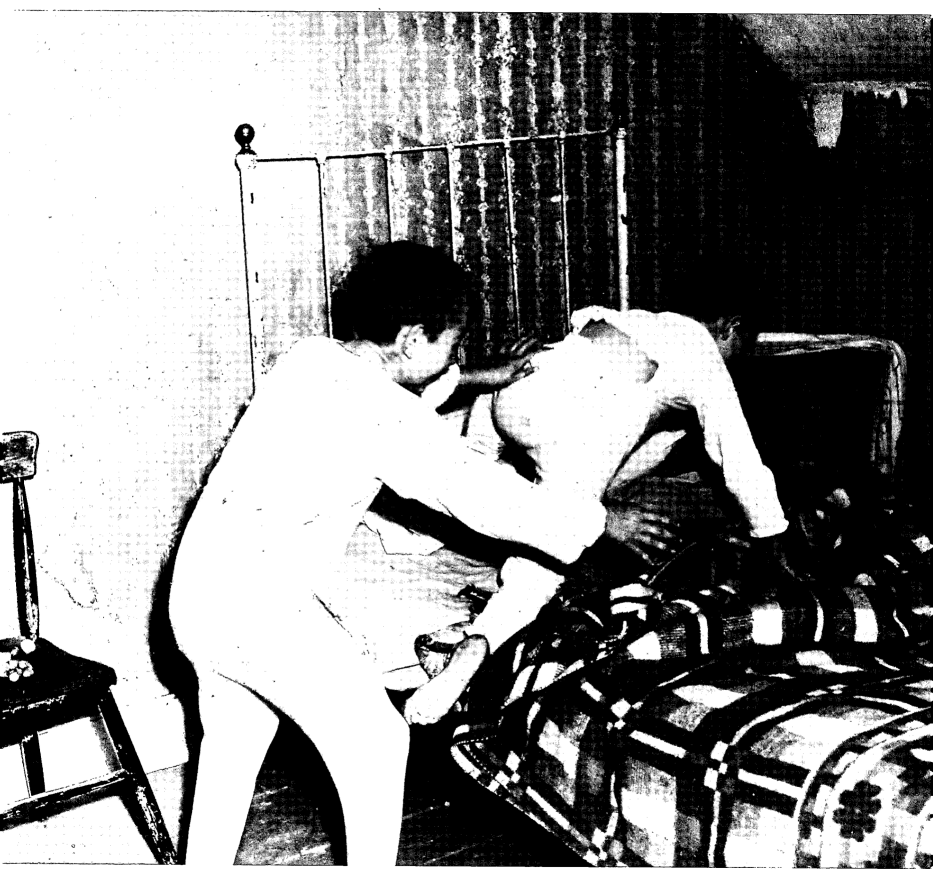

139

*Adults play games occasionally; for children,
however, the world of the imagination is as real
as getting dressed or eating or going to
sleep. (138) These boys who lived in Fairfield,
Vermont, in the hard times of 1936 must have
made a game of jumping under the covers before
the chill of an unheated bedroom penetrated
their long underwear. (139, 141) Swinging or
chasing your brother can be just a way to work
off energy, or it can be part of the imagined life of
a fireman or a pirate captain. (140) Holding the
hilltop bunker of grandfather's porch was serious
business for these Vermont cousins.*

140

141

142

(142) *Sometimes play requires props, although the props may not always be used as you would think. An umbrella, a batik shawl, and father's hat can make a wizard's costume of awesome dignity.* (143) *Trees are marvelous territories, ideal for play—multilayered, multileveled, and leafy—where a young person can lose himself and find friends and brothers and sisters and birds and worms and butterflies and secret hollows.*

143

145

144

(144–146) *One day the play shifts from the realm of fairy tales and castles; suddenly, with an experimental touch of rouge, with the murmur of big brother's heart, the mysterious adult world is glimpsed. A necktie and purse are acquired, and we have miniature versions of mother and father mugging for the camera.*

147

148

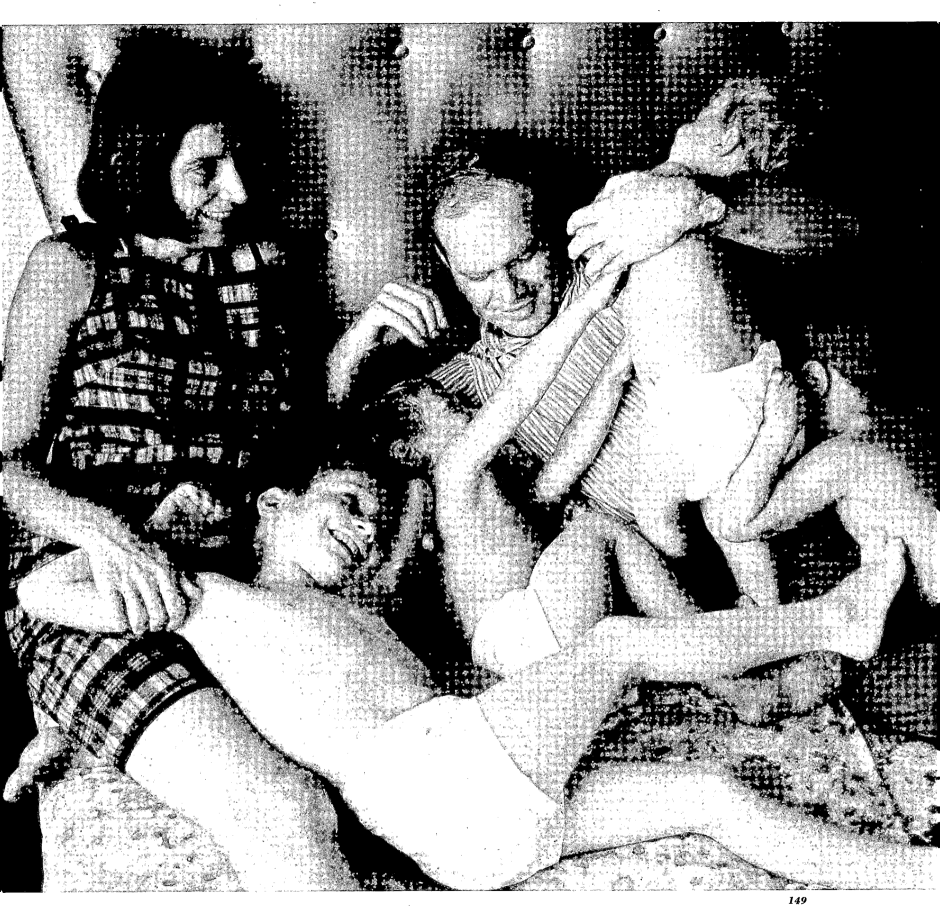

149

Organized play was something our ancestors knew little about. (147) Today, Little League lines small people up, straight as soldiers, and gives them a taste of grown-up competition and rewards. (148) Sometimes life gives the bonus of a good laugh; here several families at an amusement park find something that tickles them, and they laugh together just as the Dakins did so long ago in that parlor in Cherry Valley (128). (149) At times, something spontaneously happens to people living together in the same house, and everybody ends up together in a giggling, tickled heap.

Adolescence

"It was as if she were keeping a boarding house in a bad dream, and the children she had loved were turning into awful lodgers—lodgers who paid no rent, whose leases could not be terminated." That is how the housewife-heroine of a popular modern novel feels about her adolescent son and daughter, and that is how many of us today regard adolescence—as a metamorphosis at best, and as the occupation of home territory by hostile troops at worst. If you are a teenager, the hostile troops are your parents; if you are a parent, they are your children. In either case, adolescents' interests and parents' interests are separate and distinct, and often oppose each other.

This was not always so. In fact, there was no such period as adolescence, until recently. The stage of life to which we give that label was half recognized as "youth." but youth had been one of the traditional ages of man. It stood in its own place in a series with its own duties and obligations. Youth came just before maturity, as an anteroom in which the concerns of maturity were visible and waiting. Now adolescence seems to postpone maturity as often as it heralds its advent.

The seventeenth-century "youth" of North and South had obligations and beliefs that would have made adolescence as we know it an impossibility. In most of Western Europe and America, until the Industrial Revolution, when new mills and mines and markets made new jobs for all working people and gave them an alternative to life on the farm or, more rarely, in a small usually inherited business or trade, a child's hope for his future well-being—enough to eat and enough to wear—as well as his hope for a good spouse and a good name were bound up in the family business. There was seldom another place to go and no place where you were as important as you were at home. Even if you planned or hoped to leave home eventually, the farm or business you might set up in Ohio would probably be much the same as your father's in Massachusetts. And, if you were a girl, you would have to have your mother's skills, no matter where you went or whom you married. Therefore, it was in the interest of an adolescent to learn how to imitate, not to learn how to be independent. And his parents had had to learn how to imitate theirs, and so on, as far back as the first boat landing on this continent, and as far as memory could reach in Europe. There was no struggle between the generations, except perhaps over the specific date when parents would give up the farm, or over when the adolescent was contributing enough to make his bringing home a wife worthwhile. There was no conflict of basic interests; everyone wanted the farm to do well.

In America this coincidence of interests has always been tempered more often by other alternatives than it was in Europe. In the Old World, as Edward Shorter points out, community interests were similar, too, and reinforced the aims of each particular family. European communities were more closely knit physically, and the land was all accounted for. The possibilities of change and advancement were very limited. Consequently, it was to the advantage of everyone to work together and prosper. But in America, the community did not have the power it had in Europe because American communities were—from almost the beginning—fluid. On the rockbound coast of Puritan New England, in the deep forests of Wisconsin, and on the trackless prairies of Nebraska, community support and help were indeed welcome and sometimes essential, but nowhere were work parties formed as mutual efforts for the good of a static, defined community with defined goals, inhabited by families who had lived and would presumably live there for generations. In America, the nuclear family was more important than the extended family, who were likely to be scattered all over the road to the West, and much more important than the community, which was likely to be only one of

(150, 151) *The energy of youth and its desire to break loose from the restraints of convention were evident even in the 1880s when these youngsters—wing collars, bustles, and all—jumped over a tennis net in upstate New York. Photographing such antics was rare in the days before fast-shuttered cameras.*

several that a family had lived in. The similarity of interests between the generations in that nuclear family was not reinforced by community interests, and those interests were *generally* similar (how to run a good farm) rather than specifically similar (how to run the *same* good farm).

With the Industrial Revolution, in both Europe and America, the interests of the generations began to diverge. At first, however, even when younger members of the family did leave to work in industry, no conflict of interest was perceived because leaving home to work was in the tradition of "exchange" training that had been customary in Europe for generations. In medieval times, aristocratic households had regularly exchanged children to be brought up as squires and ladies-in-waiting to the knights and ladies of another family. The young person acquired wider experience and had the benefit of training as well. With the rise of the middle class in the merchant guilds of the cities, this practice percolated downward, and poorer families sent their boys and girls to be apprentices and "bound girls" in the shops and farms around their own homes. An apprentice worked for a master tradesman for a stated period of years, usually seven, and in return for his labor he learned his master's trade. A bound girl was indentured to a housewife, again under contract, and learned how to drudge with no such clearcut future as an apprentice could look forward to. In both cases, the young people were learning how to live as their parents might have lived.

The way in which the labor and careers of offspring fitted into the context of their parents' lives—even when the work was not identical—is demonstrated by a glorious early experiment of the Industrial Revolution at the mills of Lowell, Massachusetts. A model mill community was founded in Lowell in 1821. Afraid of establishing a debased proletariat but eager to cash in on new English weaving machinery, the founders of Lowell set up factories and clean boardinghouses, run by respectable widows. Then they recruited young women from the New England villages nearby who would come to work in the mills, hear lectures, get good food and care, and return home in a few years with money to get married on or to send a brother to college with. These Lowell mill girls, of whom Charles Dickens said on his visit in 1842, "I cannot recall or separate one young face that gave me a painful impression; not one young girl . . . whom I would have removed from those works if I had had the power," labored in order to have a better life at home with their families, not in order to separate themselves from their families. The Lowell experiment did not survive the mid-nineteenth-century influx of immigrant laborers who formed the very kind of proletariat that the original community hoped to avoid creating. And, indeed, it was among these immigrants who started their American life with subsistence-level pay for hard labor—but whose children would find jobs in middle-class trades—that the separation of parents' and childrens' interests began.

Still, for most of the nineteenth century, in the middle-class majority of the country, whether young people were farmers' daughters, preachers' sons, or the children of city office-workers, they didn't leave home. In the urban community of Union Park, Illinois, at the end of the century, young people did not leave the nest until they married, even when they were independently employed in industry. Statistical studies, done by sociologist Richard Sennett, showed that "the point of breaking from a parent's home was for the purpose of getting married," and, "a young man stayed within the orbit of his family until he was ready to found the same orbit with himself in a different position—rather like playing the same game with the players changed."

These adolescents who were striking out on their own in the nineteenth century as far as work and finances went, but leaving their hearts at home, were unaware, for the most part, of the independent behavior their work or their very bodies might lead to. American youth went on hayrides, picnics, and sleighing parties with only the slightest supervision. The importance of romantic love as a motive for marriage played a part here. Historian Frederick Lewis Allen quotes Henry Canby as saying there seemed to be around 1900

> a free association of boys and girls in their teens and early twenties that perhaps never has existed on the same plane elsewhere in the history of the modern world. We had confidence in each other and we were confided in. All through the Adirondack woods we climbed together in summer, sleeping in cabins, girls on one side, boys on the other, following by couples all day lonely and difficult trails, and in the winter skated far-off ponds, or sat all night in the spring on moonlit Delaware hills, falling in and out of love with never a crude pang of sex, though in a continual amorous excitement which was sublimated from the grosser elements of love.

174   The two important elements of modern adolescent life—peer groups and sexual interest—were critical

elements of adolescent life in the nineteenth century also, but in a different way than today. Then, the peer group imitated the adult world—it was not a besieged fort holding its own against the adult world, as it is often today—and the sexual interest was channeled in the direction of marriage, not admitted as an open element of an adolescent's present life.

Toward the end of the nineteenth century, adolescence came to be recognized as a time of flux as much as one of preparation. Henry Ward Beecher, the brother of Harriet Beecher Stowe and most illustrious minister of his era, wrote tentatively but knowledgeably about adolescent impulses in his *Lectures to Young Men*. "A young man knows little of life; less of himself. He feels in his bosom the various impulses, wild desires, restless cravings he can hardly tell for what, a sombre melancholy when all is gay, a violent exhilaration when others are sober." But Beecher's manic youngster had to beware, for at this time of life he was "exceedingly liable to be seduced into the wrong paths—into those fascinating but fatal ways, which lead to degradation and wretchedness."

The possibility of "degradation" as well as the influence of peer groups shot upward after World War I. The 1920s were, more than any other decade before the 1960s, the era of the adolescent. With 50 percent of the population living in cities in 1920, the old similarity of interests between generations, as well as the stable, rural world that fostered those interests, had largely disappeared. Also, with the increasing specialization in skills required in industry and business, higher education became a prerequisite for most youngsters. Before 1910, approximately 75 percent of the young people in America left school after eighth grade or better; in 1930, 57 percent of the population had a high-school diploma, at least. These youngsters who were not working did not see themselves as part of the adult world but lived in a socially recognized state of suspension between the child's helplessness and the adult's responsibility. In the old days, those pure groups gamboling through the Adirondacks were granted a season or two at most before they went to work and performed the duties of full-fledged adults. After 1920, prevented from any real contact with "life" for ten years or more after puberty, young people constituted a self-contained group in society. After the carnage of World War I, and in the disappointment of its aftermath, this group came to distrust the older generation. An article in the *Atlantic Monthly* of September 1920 stated, "The older generation had certainly pretty well ruined this world before passing it on to us. They give us this thing, knocked to pieces, leaky, red-hot, threatening to blow up; and then they are surprised that we don't accept it with the same attitude of pretty, decorous enthusiasm with which they received it, way back in the 'eighties." This adolescent and many others were able to feel self-righteous about breaking away from parental teachings; they could feel self-righteous all right, but they couldn't feel sure. With the independence and importance of the peer group came the generation gap and the agonizing insecurities of braces, pimples, and dates. Adolescents in the 1790s and 1890s knew what they were supposed to do—work just like everybody else—and what they weren't supposed to do—let "amorous excitement" lead to anything more than spooning. But adolescents in the 1920s and after were supposed to be adults—something that they hadn't been taught how to be. They had to learn how by trial and error.

Some parents have tried to smooth the road to adolescence by supervising their children's independent steps; historian Mary Cable has said that in the 1960s, "some mothers encourage[d] boy-girl parties, with dancing and kissing games for children in the fifth grade." But this was not ultimately satisfactory because the parents couldn't follow their children's progress very far. From the 1920s on, "petting parties" took place in that mobile den of vice, the automobile. Worse yet, when their parents tried to be like the kids, the kids felt that their last prop had been knocked out from under them. For the first time in history, perhaps, the adolescent's peer group became more important than his family. Peer groups had been important in the good old innocent nineteenth century but primarily as an energy outlet and hunting ground for future mates. After World War I, peer groups became a retreat, a world of their own. "Everybody's doing it" was first an excuse and then a dictum.

Ritual is always important for groups setting up new allegiances, and ritual has prescribed the behavior of adolescent peer groups from the 1920s to the present as strictly as ever a chaperon dictated what went on in a Victorian parlor. The fact that twentieth-century adolescent ritual was laid out by the group itself, rather than their elders, made it all the more capricious and inflexible. Novelist Lisa Alther, in her very witty novel *Kinflicks,* charts the ritualistic progress of the heroine's 1950s high-school romance with the school athletic star, Joe Bob Sparks. On their first date, "We each nodded to ourselves in satisfaction that the other, when not disguised as flag swinger or tailback, looked clean and pressed and identical to every other member of the

175

Hullsport High student body—with the exception of the hoods like Clem Cloyd, in their unspeakable tight studded blue jeans with pegged legs, and black ankle boots and dark T-shirts and windbreakers." Then, at a drive-in movie date, the exploratory physical stage of the relationship arrived—an almost obligatory step when attending a movie: "That evening, of course, opened the floodgates of groping. During the next several months, we groped all over each other—from putting our arms around each other timidly, to prim kisses with tightly closed lips, to wet messy gasping kisses with tongues intertwined and teeth clashing like rival bulls' horns." The escalation of the relationship was strictly programmed, however, according to the other rituals of high-school life. Each new sports season signaled a new physical intimacy: "He finally got around to touching my breasts, such as they were, one night after a game against the Davy Crockett Pioneers of Roaring Fork, Kentucky. By now we had hurtled into basketball season. . . . By the time baseball season arrived, anything above the waist was fair ball, so to speak."

While the young person is painfully but often ecstatically blundering around among his pretend-grown-up peer group, he encounters challenges that were insoluble for his parents and in his untapped strength, he judges his parents harshly for what seem to be their failures. At the same time, the parent, who sees his child walk into traps, unconscious of where his actions may lead, feels as though he were immured behind a thick glass wall, unable to prevent the certain disaster he sees coming. The reassessment of the child as an adult and the consequent reassessment of him as a family member that begins during adolescence can be extremely painful for everyone involved. Eventually, most families find that they have been moving toward the end of the wall, as they watched—or studiously ignored—each other, and parents come to a reunion with the child as a full-fledged adult who can be accepted by them as such and who can appreciate them for what they are.

For the last forty years peer groups have not only dictated behavior for young people but found increasing power—especially buying power—in the world at large. From the galoshes and letter sweaters of the flappers and their sheiks, through the zoot suits, and ankle socks of the 1940s and 1950s, to the denim and suede fringe of today, clothing fads among adolescents were matched *and* exceeded by the changing dance crazes of the Charleston, the Lindy, the Twist, the Frug, and the Hustle. The record business grew into a multimillion-dollar enterprise and made the careers of singers from Frank Sinatra and Elvis Presley to the Beatles and Joni Mitchell. Adolescents evolved their own slang, which became dated and unusable just about the time that the adult world caught on to it, and adolescents had a great deal to do with keeping forbidden liquor, in the 1920s, and forbidden marijuana, in the 1960s, in circulation.

In the 1960s the Vietnam War drove the wedge even deeper between generations than World War I had done, and the adolescent sub-culture—at least its older members—found an ideology to justify its separate life style: It was right to live in communes and smoke pot because the adults who condemned these things were responsible for killing helpless Vietnamese babies with napalm. Even in relatively conservative areas of the country, the split between age groups has recently been marked by small differences in life style.

Sociologist Edward Shorter says that in the 1960s the relationship between parents and adolescent children became one of "friendship" rather than "function." In Shorter's terms, a relationship of friendship is nonessential and maintained by choice, whereas a functional relationship is maintained by necessity. One aspect of contemporary teenage-parent relations that Shorter perhaps ignores—and which hampers the workings of "friendship"—is teenagers' financial dependence—no matter how distinct their life style and no matter how powerful their sub-culture—on their parents. The reins are slack, but young people are still attached to the family buggy.

It is hard for everyone today—parents, children, bachelors, widows—to know how to live. The old patterns are breaking down under pressure from the new technology that renders those patterns meaningless. From day to day, there appear new gadgets, new mores, new holes in the social fabric to be dealt with. People in their middle years may cope better than teenagers because they are more certain of themselves; on the other hand, they may not cope as well because they are less flexible. These adolescents who are being catapulted into adulthood by early sexual experience, the availability of drugs, and the pressures to produce in school are explorers charting country they have never seen before. Their findings may help us all.

(152) Until after World War I, when compulsory education was extended in many states to the age of sixteen, most adolescents simply worked as adults, helping to support the family. This boy gives his father a hand at the grindstone.

Before American psychologist G. Stanley Hall wrote a weighty two-volume study called Adolescence in 1904, teenagers were treated alternately as children and as adults, but were not thought of as living through a distinct stage of life. (153) In 1914 a New York City pair, only fifteen despite the grown-up togs, were tagged by a younger brother, perhaps envious of their sophistication on skates. (154) Girls and boys were trained early in grown-up manners. These well-to-do children in their white dresses and Eton jackets attended dancing class on Staten Island when it was still a haunt of country gentry, around 1895. (155) The Hanlon sisters lived with their widowed mother and maiden aunts, the Misses Cochrane, in the little mill town of Monongahela, Pennsylvania, where they were photographed sitting by the wisteria vine on the front porch in 1912. The clothes of the girls, Margaret, bottom center, then, counterclockwise, Frances and Louise, show how childhood imperceptibly merged into adulthood, with slowly lengthening skirts and hair put up with gradually smaller ribbons. There were no separate styles for adolescents—just a compromise between children's garb and grown-ups'.

153

154

After World War I, adolescents went to work later and lived their own semi-independent lives at school longer than ever before. (157) Smoking and the "boyish bob" haircut were two of the daring new styles girls took up in the 1920s; petting and drinking illegal hooch were two more temptations that these four slick young California women, posing with three boys at a swimming pool, were susceptible to. (156) In Boothville, Louisiana, in 1938 it was painfully important, as it has been for teenagers for fifty years, to be just like everybody else in their gang. In that place at that time, wearing straw "boaters" was the key to belonging, although the youth standing up seems to have some doubts about membership in the club. (158) Twenty years later in New Jersey, beehive hairdos were the rage; from the security of their clique these girls looked with suspicion on the hostile world of rival gangs and the opposite sex.

156

159

160

(159, 160) *In 1964 in Cleveland, the prescribed costume for teenage dates was madras shirts, cut-off jeans, and circle pins. The prescribed place for a date, if it wasn't a school dance or the local pizza parlor, was the drive-in movie, where the movie was less of an attraction than your date. The automobile has been the great testing ground of adult behavior for adolescents for the last fifty years. In the old days, the social arenas were the family-supervised parlor and dancing school.*

161

An adolescent becomes especially aware of family
pressures when at the point of asserting his
independence, and the older family members may
feel that they have failed when this product of their
own flesh suddenly chooses a road they can't
follow. (161) Rob Smith of Vermont wanted to leave
a family party on his father's new boat to attend a
dance, and his father complained, only
half-jokingly, "You're leaving me alone with my
new toy." (162) A woman of Italian descent, a
people traditionally possessive of their offspring,
seems to disapprove of her son and his girlfriend's
behavior, which the young people, in turn,
exaggerate in her presence. (163) Confusion at
losing control was expressed by this New England
grandmother, who said as her teenage
granddaughter described a new bathing suit, "I
didn't raise your father to let you wear things like
that. You'll just have to get a little vest to cover up
those dreadful empty spaces."

162

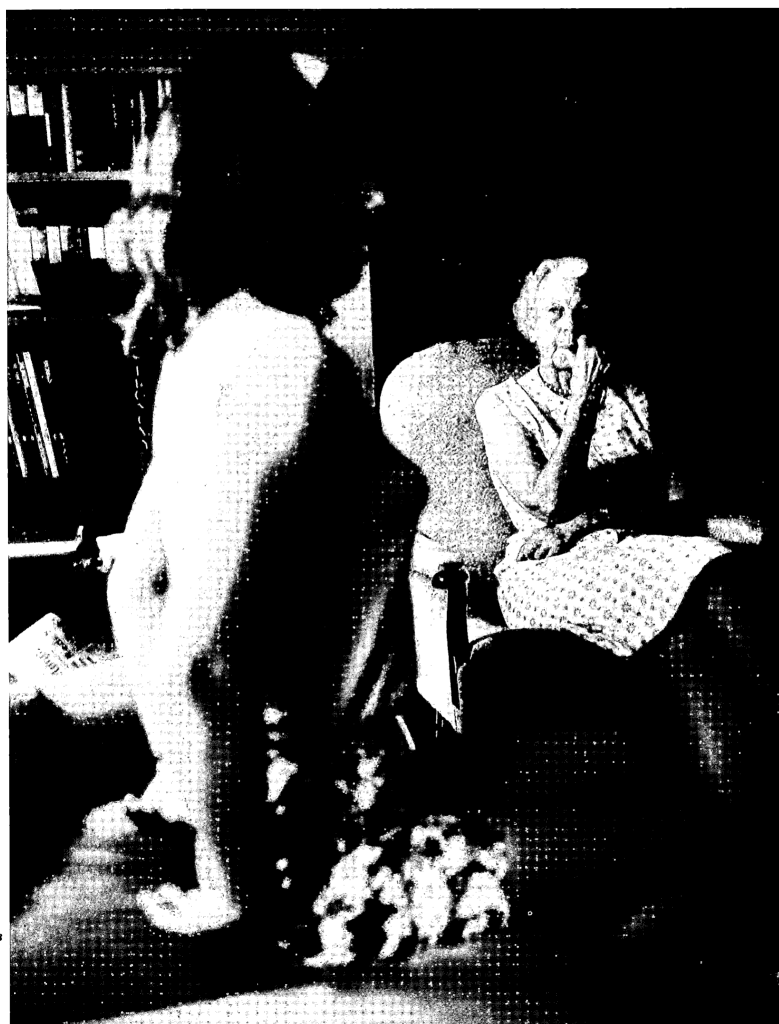

The adolescent is torn between identifying with his peers and identifying with the adults he knows best—his parents. Bill Owens's photograph of a father and son in California (164) has as much to say about the generations' conflicting desires as do the subjects' opinions of the picture: "Basically we are very much alike, the same individual. Our temperaments, however, are different, we reflect on things differently. My son was raised to think for himself"; and, "My father is an ex-Army officer, I'm an ex-Marine. My lifestyle changes were hard for my dad to understand. I'm a freer individual, not different. He doesn't understand that." (165) The 1960s youth community, whose members advised each other to "tune in, turn on, and drop out," was the most developed form so far of the peer groups that had been absorbing more and more of adolescents' attention since the 1920s. (166) Daisy Boone of North Carolina lived in a log cabin with her mother in the 1960s and broke her foot "joy-riding" on the way home from a dance. Convalescent, she posed beside her mother, her cigarettes and makeup emphasizing the difference between them, although the linked hands indicate the continuity of family line from woman to woman.

164

165

Grandparents

The most famous American, known as the Father of His Country, was also our first famous grandfather. George Washington accepted the responsibility of raising his step-grandchildren, George Washington Parke Custis and Eleanor Parke Custis, in 1781, when their father (the son of Washington's wife, by whom he never had any children of his own) died at the close of the Revolutionary War. His stepson had been a disappointment to Washington, who deplored his frivolity and indolence.

The grandchildren came to Mount Vernon at a time when the general's own prominence in the new nation took much of his time and attention. Nonetheless, there are various portraits of George in his uniform and Martha in her mobcap in the portico at Mount Vernon, attended by two young Custises, wearing the same smart clothes as the children of Marie Antoinette, their contemporaries, along with rather stiff public expressions.

Washington's prestige was awesome by that time, but his authority suffered with his grandchildren as it had with his stepson, from the effects of Martha's indulgence and his grandson's indolence. But Nelly Custis was playful and affectionate with him; she sang for the many state visitors who came to dinner and arranged to be married on February 22, 1799, her grandfather's last birthday, as it proved.

Although his relationship with his grandchildren was not satisfactory in every respect to the head of the family, it impressed the American public as supremely so. The rather remote but kindly figure who has the pillar of experience and community approbation supporting him was many people's notion of what a grandparent should be for the first 150 years of the republic. Even Washington's failings on the side of indulgence fit in with the current idea that a grandparent might choose to be lenient with his grandchildren—perhaps even spoil them. For many years, grandparents were traditionally considered a refuge in time of trouble, a last authority, and conservers of the family traditions. It has been a long, long step down off that pillar for the modern grandparent who is too often thought of as dependent, or pictured as kept around the house on sufferance or placed with considerate rejection in a nursing home.

The traditional American view of the grandparent was probably seldom borne out in fact, however, even in earlier times. In the late eighteenth century in America and Europe, the average lifespan for men and women was only thirty-five to forty years. Fewer people survived into their fifties and sixties to function as active grandparents, and so, particularly on a farm where all hands were useful, a grandparent was likely to be a help and also a valuable source of knowledge in the community. This did give grandparents social significance, but what reduced their power in the family sharply was the mobility that Americans engaged in. Until the late nineteenth century, whenever families felt constricted, the younger members simply up and went West. Today, the reasons for the generations' breaking apart are somewhat different, but the ease with which it is done remains nearly the same, and it is estimated that, contrary to our preconceptions, no more than 10 percent of elderly Americans have ever lived with their grown children and grandchildren. Moreover, most accounts of family life surviving from the late eighteenth and early nineteenth centuries that portray a grandparent as a benign, revered despot were written by prosperous people, the only ones with sufficient education, leisure, and interest to record their memoirs. When a grandparent has economic clout, he is most likely to be evident and remembered. Poorer grandparents of earlier times were apt to have poorer grandchildren, who had no time or inclination to scribble about the old days at home, when a grandparent was, if not a burden, at least another mouth to feed, like every other family member.

(167) In 1905 a Wisconsin grandmother, looking prouder than she wanted to admit, clutched the hand of a reluctant little boy who wore the dress put on all small children. The bicycle belonged to a father or big brother, and perhaps it was he who carefully took the picture.

One severe blow to the ideal of the authoritarian grandparent—and it seems to have been a popular ideal, however much or little it was reflected in real life—came with the first floods of non-English-speaking immigrants in the mid-nineteenth century. The German immigrants of the eighteenth century had kept their culture pretty well intact from generation to generation, probably because of a combination of circumstances involving poor language communication with other settlers and the distinct "plain" style of life prompted by their religious beliefs. But when the Scandinavians and a second wave of Germans came in the 1850s, followed by Poles, Slovaks, Italians, Greeks, and Chinese at the end of the century, the most profound of generation gaps were about to be dug. Within ten or fifteen years of the immigrants' arrival, their grown children, who had been partially assimilated into the surrounding culture, would get married and have children of their own, who would perhaps not even speak the same language their grandparents spoke. In 1890, 76 percent of the white population of New York City had foreign-born mothers; in another ten years, their children would often find it difficult to treat the foreign-born grandmothers as anything other than ludicrous, kerchiefed relics, let alone authority figures.

Heartbreaking failures of understanding occurred when immigrant grandparents' cherished reserves of knowledge, along with the habits that gave the only stability there was to their uprooted lives, were derided by their children and simply ignored by their grandchildren. A Sicilian-born writer reminiscing about his upbringing in Rochester, New York, around 1900 remarked sadly: "If the children had had their own way, my parents would have dropped all their Sicilian ideas and customs and behaved more like other Americans. That was our childhood dream. Yet, as much as we wanted them to be Americans and as much as we wanted to live an American life, we did not have the vaguest notion as to how to go about it." Not knowing how to go about it produced such humiliating misunderstandings as that of a small Italian boy who told his school class how teeth could be kept white. His teacher had praised his, and when he asked his parents—at her request—what kept teeth white (since he had never been to a dentist), they summoned up the remembrance of an uncle whose strong teeth were maintained by rinsing them occasionally with his own urine. His prescription was not received well.

On the other hand, if immigrant children were embarrassed by the encumbrance of outdated folkways, their parents felt abandoned and humiliated by their children. A Russian Jewess wrote at the turn of the century to the personal advice column of the *Forward,* the New York Yiddish-language newspaper about her daughter, who "married a Hungarian-Jewish young man [whom she had met in New York]. She adopted all the Hungarian customs and not a trace of a Russian-Jewish woman remained with her. This would not have been so bad. The trouble is, now that she is first-class Hungarian, she laughs at the way I talk, at my manners, and even the way we cook."

Sometimes there was a happy outcome when immigrants who were rejected by their children—or felt themselves to be so—maintained cultural values or customs that eventually interested their grandchildren. A *New York Times* book reviewer has said of the immigrant experience that "the first generation tries to retain as much as possible, the second to forget, the third to remember," and the source of the remembrance was a grandparent who could recall the feel of the Russian snow or the odor of the steerage compartment in the ship coming to America. The need to keep in touch with one's own past was articulated by writer Herbert Gold. "What my father has left me of my grandfather is a silent old man with a long white beard, a horse, a cart, a cow, a mud-and-log house—an old-country grandfather fixed in my mind like the memory of a painting. That's not enough, of course. This stylization of images does not satisfy the cravings for history. I must try to tempt out the truth."

The "truth" will probably be absorbing and memorable to a child whether it comes from a grandmother who tells in broken English of a pogrom in a Russian village or from a grandfather of a long-settled family who takes his small grandson downtown to see the nick in the bank's doorframe that his great-grandfather made when he threw his inkwell at an unscrupulous politician trying to extort a loan. A man who grew up in western Pennsylvania remembers his grandfather taking him when he was six years old along a path covered with sodden leaves to a stone foundation deep in the woods—all that remained of the house where the grandfather himself was born. The old man showed the little boy several blunt, rusty iron nails and said those were what had held the house together; he also said that when he was as small as his grandson, his family had had to ford the creek in five places in order to get to town, and in winter the water splashed on the horses' fetlocks froze and sounded like sleigh bells. That vivid glimpse of a vanished commonplace fact of life remained with the grandson for years.

When grandparents are able to communicate some sense of what the past was like, they help to place the child in what has been called the "generational chain." The child realizes, although dimly when he is young, that he is part of a context and that his behavior and very personality are not unique. The grandparent has the satisfying vision of his grandchild carrying on cultural traditions and also the self-affirming vision of his grandchild expressing traits of behavior—good and not so good—that the grandparent has seen before. In *Manchild in the Promised Land*, Claude Brown talks about the time he spent on the Southern farm where his grandparents, black sharecroppers, had labored all their lives. Brown's grandfather was well known—and even respected—in the community because he had been "a real bad and evil nigger when he was a young man" and wouldn't knuckle under to circumstances. Once, when young Brown was playing with a cousin, and the boys tried to lift heavy sacks of corn, Brown's grandmother came flying out of the cabin and whipped him. Later, she explained in a roundabout way that his grandpa had once tried to carry a still out from under the noses of the revenue men and given himself a hernia as a result. "She was saying that she didn't mean to hit me. She just didn't want me to break my window [get a hernia] . . . I knew I had fallen in love with that mean old wrinkled lady who, I used to think, had a mouth like a monkey. I had fallen in love with a mean old lady because she hit me across the neck for trying to lift a sack of corn." Through this confrontation, Claude Brown, who was already aware of the authority and presence his grandfather had in the community, was also made rather abruptly aware that his grandmother was frightened that he might have his grandfather's self-destructive wilfulness, as well as his independence. For a grandparent, the vision of a grandchild carrying on his own life, prolonging it in a sense, can be both frightening and appealing.

The grandparent enjoys a relationship with a child who is part of his bone and blood, for whom he did not have to suffer birth pains and for whom he, usually, does not have to suffer expense or discipline worries. The grandparent can indulge himself as well as the child when they are together. When a tolerant grandmother takes a small child to the city to shop, for instance, she usually promises a new toy, which doesn't have to fit into the family budget, which is chosen after loving and lingering attention—time that doesn't have to be snatched from marketing. Then, after the toy has been picked by the child and paid for by Grandma and carried off in a firm grasp, both the elderly purchaser and the young recipient can repair to a tea room. There an orgy of nourishment can take place which may consist of dishes refused by the child at home (chicken salad, olives) but consumed here because there's no coercion involved and dishes frowned on at home (Coca-Cola, hot fudge sundaes) but allowed here because it's a treat and Grandma won't have to clean up if the child gets sick. Here are love and attention, with no responsibility extending beyond the afternoon—the best fantasy of romance doesn't ask for more.

The typical modern grandparent, whose relationship with a grandchild includes such magic shopping trips, occupies a position that defines itself somewhere between the autocratic patriarch or matriarch and the dependent relative. In talking about the contemporary grandparent, sociologists Bernice Neugarten and Karol Weinstein make a distinction between the "formal" grandparent, "who may occasionally take on a minor service such as baby-sitting [but] maintain[s] clearly demarcated lines between parenting and grandparenting," and the "fun-seeker," who "joins the child in specific activities for the specific purpose of having fun, somewhat as if he were the child's playmate." Both of these are distinct from the "surrogate parent," who is usually a grandparent living in the home. In the first two categories are the 84 percent of the American population over sixty-five years old who live less than an hour away from one of their children but do live separately from them. These independent grandparents—who are in the position that countless interviews and common sense together indicate most older people desire—can have direct contact with their grandchildren, in almost whatever mode they choose, with a minimum of parental interference.

When a grandparent does live in the home with children and grandchildren, the grandparent is sometimes the mainstay of the family, providing an invaluable extra pair of hands in helping with the children and housework. Until recently, many black families were dependent emotionally on a matriarchal grandmother, who reared a second generation, often while she was still the financial and domestic support of her own children. Often, however, a grandparent living with younger generations provides a focus for conflict in which someone's independence is lost; either the children feel financially dependent on the grandparent and

191

do not fully pursue their own careers and relationships, or the grandparent finds himself in an emotionally or financially dependent position and is relegated to second-class citizenship in the home. Although we are tempted to see this dilemma as a product of modern small houses and frequent mobility, the low percentage of grandparents living with their children throughout American history suggests that cohabitation has often been a problem.

Most successfully, it seems safe to suggest, do those grandparents function who can sit serenely distant from the grandchild and offer stability and continuity while deriving pleasure from the child's growth and change. They need not themselves change with the child, as parents must, and indeed their value lies in being an entity as dependable in an emotional way as the sugar cookies they produce are culinarily.

This dependability, and the grandparent's value as a link to the past, comes partly from the grandchild's difficulty in imagining an older grandparent as ever having been young. Glenway Westcott, in *The Grandmothers,* notes this common feeling on the part of a child. "He seemed scarcely human to his grandson—an old ghost of another epoch, a ghost which, even in its youth, could not have been very young." There seems to a young grandchild no resemblance whatsoever between the old person he sees sitting in a chair beside an unnecessary fire that overheats the room and the yellowing photograph, pasted on brown cardboard, of a dapper young man with his hat pushed back on black curly hair or the snapshot of a young girl in a white dress with a high collar. And yet, no matter how young the grandchild, he knows that he is connected to that very old, wrinkled person and so concludes that, after all, the old person must be connected to the youth in the photograph, and so it goes, like leapfrog, with each generation jumping imaginatively over an old grandparent back into the grandparent's youth—and into the past and the history of the family.

(168) *Passing on traditions can be important for a grandfather, who finds a kind of immortality through his descendant, and for a grandchild, too, who comprehends the past through an old person. On Memorial Day in the late 1800s, Civil War veterans like this old warrior of the Grand Army of the Republic always marched to the cemetery. The little boy examines his grandfather's flag and the flowers the old man carried to adorn veteran and family graves.*

Grandchildren, at least for middle-class grandparents, are more often a joy than a burden, but the black tradition of shifting marriages has often left grandparents responsible for the upbringing of their children's children at a time in life when people most need rest themselves. (169) A new grandchild seems to give a turn-of-the-century grandmother back her youth—the time when she cared for her own children. (170) These happy people who resemble each other, and the dog that the old lady is determined will pose, suggest the joy that different generations can find together. Families seem now to have been happier as a unit before World War I, when they shared the same expectations of life and of each other from generation to generation. (171) Photographer Frances Benjamin Johnson, traveling through the South in 1902, photographed a country family in their cabbage patch. The grandmother seems resigned to caring for yet another new baby, whom she must feed and dress in dearly earned, clean, starched clothes.

169

170

To young people, grandparents seem to offer an abundance of good things that seems limitless. There is usually more liberty, more attention, more pocket money, and, of course, more favorite food at Grandma's than anybody offers at home. (172) In the 1950s this plump grandmother still used an old-fashioned stove to provide one of those belly-stretching dinners that growing boys need. One dinner his Pennsylvania grandmother served the author on a broiling July day many years ago consisted of chicken and dumplings, mashed potatoes, sauerkraut, hot biscuits, and lemon sponge pie. (173) An old gentleman of Muncie, Indiana, put his little granddaughter on the counter at Wade's Greenhouse one afternoon in 1936.(174) At the Cotton Carnival Picnic in Hayti, Missouri, in July 1942, home-baked treats and "store bread" were jumbled together on the family's cloth. A young man, whose older brothers may have been away at war, shared his taste for the all-American Coke with his grandmother.

172

173

174

(175–79) *Photographer Cornell Capa did a photographic essay in 1959 on the life of a Philadelphia grandmother who lived with her son (a factory foreman), his wife, and seven children in a six-room house. Annie Mahaffey was eighty years old. She had been a widow for nineteen years, and she loved and squabbled with and helped financially support the family she was part of. The family's remarks about themselves at the time were clear-sighted and only partly complaining. (176) Annie said, "I know I have a bad temper, but I only tell them how I would do it. Can't I open my mouth?" About her son, she offered, "George, he's the best of them, but he's between two women." (178) The other woman, Annie's daughter-in-law Mary, seconded the opinion of George from her own point of view. "You know, I'm the envy of every girl on the block because of George, the way he is toward me and the children." Occasionally Annie lapsed into self-pity. "They're all going to miss me when I'm dead and gone," she would say. And it was probably true.*

177

175

176

180

181

The situation of a grandparent in a
retirement or nursing home is just the
opposite of Annie Mahaffey's. Contact with
grandchildren may be joyful and briefly
fulfilling, but its brevity is tantalizing. The
void felt when the old person is alone again
is all the greater. (180–83) Well-off enough
financially to make her own arrangements,
this woman in a Long Island retirement
home is deprived of the rough-and-tumble
involvement that the Mahaffey household
offered Annie.

(184) *Families today are often subject to stress of their own making, but in the nineteenth century the disruption of death or disaster struck without warning and devastated people already exhausted by struggling for subsistence. In 1862, making a last attempt to defend their homeland, Sioux Indians in Minnesota under Chief Little Crow massacred eight hundred settlers in surprise attacks. Some settlers were photographed during a respite in their flight from the massacres; their faces reflect the emotional exhaustion of people who have seen family members slaughtered, suffered a forced march, and anticipate still further dangers. The irony is that Indian families had endured similar conditions for more than two centuries.*

Stress and Disruption

For the first three hundred years of American life, stress was more likely to be the result of family disruption than its cause. Today, domestic stress can lead to the total rupture of the family circle if one partner or the other decides to file for a separation. With one marriage in every three ending in divorce, stress wreaks ever more drastic damage on the family. In the days before 1920, on the contrary, marriages were made for life, most people thought, and domestic stress tended to be one of the chronic annoyances that people endured like ague or rheumatism. Really severe stress only came after the all-too-frequent disruption caused by death.

The frequency of death, which left many mothers of five or six with only two children surviving infancy and which held life expectancy down to forty years or so (for much of the eighteenth century, the average lifespan was thirty-eight years; by 1900 it had only climbed to forty-seven), made dying an object of morbid and romantic fascination. Historian Mary Cable points out that the Puritans' obsession with death came from the added awful titillation of believing that very few of their number were predestined to enjoy eternal life. Most people (they thought) had to burn throughout eternity, and this certainty was graven on their tombstones in the form of skulls and crossbones. By the mid-eighteenth century, death was no less frequent a visitor to cradle and fireside, but Americans had taken a more hopeful view of its aftermath, and waxed sentimental. Cable quotes a hymn composed by George Whiteside, an evangelist of the 1740s, which began

> Ah! Lovely appearance of death
> No sight upon earth is so fair;
> Not all the gay pageants that breathe,
> Can with a dead body compare.

This sentimentality flourished—rankly—through the nineteenth century in such forms as mourning pictures and poems like those that Huck Finn said gave him "the fantods." Mark Twain spoofed the common custom of glorifying death in the mourning pictures made by one of the Grangerford daughters, whose habits he has Huck describe: "Every time a man died, or a woman died, or a child died, she would be on hand with her 'tribute' before he was cold. She called them tributes. The neighbors said it was the doctor first, then Emmeline, then the undertaker."

Dwelling on death served a purpose, however; it helped to keep alive in memory the many who were claimed by it and helped dissipate the grief of the survivors. Families universally went into mourning, even in poor country districts, wearing black for a year at least—and, in the case of widows, for the rest of their lives. Memorial Day, originally established to honor the Civil War dead, became popular nationwide as a time to go to the local cemetery and decorate the graves of departed family members with snowball blossoms and lilacs and early roses.

The Civil War itself was one of the bitterest examples of the horror of death and disruption that wars have brought to American family life. Because Americans were fighting on both sides, the casualties were statistically staggering (540,000 killed in a population of 31 million), and sometimes the split in the Union was mirrored in individual families, whose members fought against each other. Samuel Eliot Morison, in his *Oxford History of the American People*, suggests what the war meant to various families whom we can identify—because of their prominence then or later.

> Three grandsons of Henry Clay fought for the Union, and four for the Confederacy. Three
> brothers of Mrs. Lincoln died for the South; several kinsmen of Mrs. [Jefferson] Davis were in the
> Union army. In a house in West 20th Street, New York, a little boy named Theodore Roosevelt

prayed for the Union armies at the knee of his Georgian mother whose brothers were in the Confederate navy. At the same moment, in the Presbyterian parsonage of Augusta, Georgia, another little boy named Thomas Woodrow Wilson knelt in the family circle while his Ohio-born father invoked the God of Battles for the Southern cause.

Later wars have been less disturbing to national unity but scarcely less devastating to any family touched by death. The Vietnam War, the first that was not endorsed by almost all Americans, affected families as painfully as had the Civil War. A passage from C.D.B. Bryan's *Friendly Fire,* which examins the response of an Iowa farm couple to their son's death in Vietnam, suggests the force that a report of sudden death has on a family.

> He thought he recognized the first car as that of their parish priest, Father Otto Shimon, but that second car . . . Gene was now close enough to read black letters painted on the door of the olive-drab Chevrolet: "U.S. Army—For Official Use Only." Gene felt his chest tighten, and he stood still while the priest and an Army sergeant stepped out of their cars and slammed the doors shut. . . .
>
> Not until the priest looked up did Gene recognize the fright, the despair, the agony in his eyes, and then, very quietly, he asked, "Is my boy dead?" . . .
>
> Peg Mullen heard the back door open, heard Gene rush into the kitchen, heard him shout, *"It's Mikey! It's Mikey!"*—his voice half a sob, half a scream.

The nineteenth-century attitude toward death, which seems mawkish to us, may have helped families deal with its terrible presence by giving them forms and manners for such confrontations.

As the nineteenth century was fascinated with death as a cause of domestic devastation, so divorce has a glitter of horrid fascination and repulsion for us. But until the twentieth century, divorce was not considered a fit subject for contemplation. It was as distasteful as murder, and as awkward, too, with a corpse that refused to decently decay and go away.

Although the ancient world had recognized divorce of various kinds (the Old Testament prescribes that a man who does not favor his wife may "write her a bill of divorcement, and give it in her hand and send her out of his house"), the Christian tradition and the medieval originators of our laws did not acknowledge the possibility of divorce at all. It remained for the Puritans, surprisingly, to make divorce less a matter of sin than a matter of occasional necessity. The Puritans insisted that each man was responsible to God for his own actions and his own government, and such government should not be made God's responsibility in the form of a churchly sacrament. If a man who had got married in a civil ceremony in colonial Massachusetts messed up his marriage, it was the responsibility of the civil government to decide whether it should be dissolved. Thus, between 1630 and 1692, there were 40 divorces in New England, whereas in England, where marriage remained a matter for the church, only 229 divorces were granted between 1700 and 1850.

Despite the relatively liberal attitude of early America toward divorce, the step was never taken or granted lightly. Though they varied from state to state, the admitted grounds for divorce were always specific and very grim: bigamy, failure to consummate the marriage, desertion, and the old reliable adultery. In all such cases, with the arguable exception of adultery, the marriage had quite literally evaporated or never existed, and divorce merely recognized the situation. Limited to these grounds, divorce was really only a refinement of the medieval church practice of annulment, which was based on the premise that a marriage could only be dissolved when there was some fundamental reason why it should never have been. Today divorce is often the final, formal step in the disintegration of what was a very real marriage.

One survival of a medieval practice that lingered on into the mid-nineteenth century was the bed-and-board divorce. In these cases, a person who had been injured in the marriage relationship was freed from living with or being financially responsible for his or her spouse, but neither party could marry again. Though intended to discourage lax sexual morality, which might tempt a husband or wife to discard a spouse without sufficient cause, in fact, the bed-and-board divorce fostered adultery by leaving healthy young men and women trapped in celibacy that was not of their own choosing. By 1870, when Massachusetts abolished bed-and-board divorce, almost all the states granted outright divorces after due legal proceedings, and the stage was set for our modern practices.

Edith Wharton wrote a short story in 1911, "Autres Temps," in which she describes a divorcée's state of mind.

> When she was alone, it was always the past that occupied her. She couldn't get away from it, and she didn't any longer care to. During her long years of exile she had made her terms with it, had learned to accept the fact that it would always be there, huge, obstructing, encumbering, bigger and more dominant than anything the future could ever conjure up. And, at any rate, she was sure of it, she understood it, knew how to reckon with it; she had learned to screen and manage and protect it as one does an afflicted member of one's family.

Had it taken place in real life, Mrs. Lidcote's fictional divorce would have been one of the rare 50,000 for that year. Its consequences then were so unpleasant and severe that Mrs. Wharton could without exaggeration have her heroine embark for Europe and not come back until twenty-five years after the event. To view a divorcée's past as though it were "an afflicted member of the family"—and the divorcée herself as someone wounded beyond healing—is particularly Victorian. Today we rather militantly insist on the possibility of recovering from divorce; indeed, anyone who persists in behaving as though he were irreparably wounded is likely to be accused of making a martyr of himself. Nonetheless, Edith Wharton's sense of divorce as a trauma, an act that profoundly affects the future, is as psychologically valid now as then.

After World war I, with changing mores and social habits, brought about in part by the shift of the American population to the cities as well as by increasing opportunities for mobility and new ease of communication, divorce became a much more common and much less discredited solution to marital unhappiness. The voices of conservatism thundered from pulpit and political platform, however, as they had and would for generations. In 1884 Timothy Dwight, president of Yale University, declaimed unequivocally that it was "incomparably better that individuals should suffer than that an Institution, which is the basis of all human good, should be shaken, or endangered." In 1934 a Catholic magazine mourned, "It is folly to say that the institution of marriage is in danger; the institution of marriage is gone." And in 1969 newspaper columnist Harriet Van Horne asked rather wildly, "Are we the last married generation? Well, if we are, prepare for anarchy, chaos and a breakdown in all the civilized amenities." In vain were such cries of outrage and despair, for Americans resolutely dissolved their marriages in ever-growing numbers from 1890, when the first divorce statistics were recorded, to the present. There was a substantial increase in the number of divorces between 1890 and 1930, and, predictably it now seems, another after World War II (when many hastily contracted wartime marriages fell apart); then the statistics fell during the placid 1950s and rose again to 660,000 divorces (compared to 2,146,000 marriages) in 1969.

The stress that brings about a divorce and what the rupture means to each family are, at the beginning, as unfathomable as the deepest currents moving through the ocean are to the naked eye. Many couples contain their anguish and the marks of disintegration within their homes until a final irrevocable break occurs, just as many people harbor the signs of cancer or heart disease for years without being aware of them until their bodies break down. Joseph Epstein tells in his lucid and provocative study *Divorced in America* of the tension that tangled him and his wife in mutual dissatisfaction, until any action by one aggravated the other. Although the context of their quarrel is contemporary, the dynamics are timeless.

> Your own life, though it seemed no great bargain to you, came to seem more interesting than hers, at least in her eyes, and when you would tell her, in the evenings, about a good restaurant you had been to for lunch that day, or about someone out of the ordinary you had met, you began to sense a subtle tinge of envy in her response. . . . So you began to hold back, the first time that you had held back anything in your marriage. . . . Since anything special in your life became an affront to hers, you determined to match her drabness for drabness in the chronicle of your days. . . . Your ambition and her boredom—these were two of the main spears in the side of your marriage. Twist one and the other turned with it. Because you earned a lot of money, she didn't have to work. Because she didn't have to work, she nearly choked on her freedom. Your money made possible her boredom. Bored, she disdained your ambition; ambitious, you grew tired of her boredom. She began to resent the time you spent at your desk; you, knowing her resentment, began to resent the time you spent away from it. Twist one spear and the other turned with it.

The weight of stress that forces the ultimate rupture can cause cracks and strains before that. Alcoholism and forms of drug addiction (sometimes stemming from dependence on tranquilizers or anti-depressants meant to help the unhappy person) may reflect insecurities that the marriage strains have accentuated and made nearly irrevocable. As the strain increases, so, of course, does the pseudo-solution of the addiction, which further increases the strain. As Epstein says, "Twist one spear and the other turns with it."

The legal process itself, with the paraphernalia of courtrooms and lawyers and judges and the dividing of possessions and awarding of alimony, opens the field to blows and thrusts of accumulated bitterness that can make a battlefield seem mercifully impersonal in comparison. In fact, the analogy between divorce and war is instructive because divorce and war are the only acts of violence—albeit psychological rather than physical in the case of divorce—that society condones, apart from game situations. Although the ease and frequency of divorce today seem to indicate that it is fully socially acceptable, the fact that it is still regarded as an antisocial act of violence can be deduced from the courtroom procedure followed today, much as it was in the age when divorce was a social crime. Bernard Weisberger points out in *American Heritage* (October 1971) that the effect of putting divorce in the courts, as happened in most states in the middle nineteenth century, "was to freeze divorce into the American judicial mold of adversary proceedings. Each divorce was a dispute to be tried, with someone to be found guilty of misconduct, instead of a no-fault investigation into a human tragedy."

For the partners in an ending marriage, as well as for the children, who are helpless passengers in the foundering enterprise (in 1967, 701,000 children had parents who were divorcing—twice as many as in 1955), the adjustment is prolonged as the separated individuals try to become used to being apart. For adults, the adjustment usually involves certain predictable reactions: relief at having made the break (with suspense and indecision over at last), pride in newly found independence, then despair at having been deserted, feelings of profound failure and intermittent inability to bear the terrible solitariness. Comparing the loneliness of divorce to that experienced by the survivors of a death in the family, Epstein wondered after his divorce, "What will it be like . . . to lose parents, friends, people you have not broken with but whom death will break first? But sometimes you wonder, thinking in the simple selfish terms of your own emotional economy, whether it is less painful to have people who were once very alive to you dead, or having dead to you people who are still very much alive?"

The loneliness caused by the death of a spouse or parent brings with it much of the sense of guilt and, however irrationally, the same sense of failure that divorce does. Many children feel that the death of a parent is somehow their fault and are quite explicit about it, as was the small boy in the well-known story: Found crying several days after his mother's death, he said that if he hadn't been bad and broken the refrigerator, maybe his mother wouldn't have died. Sociologists and psychologists say today that most people go through three stages following the death of a close family member—denial, depression, and recovery. The denial stage is somewhat comparable to the feeling of independence and self-assertion that follows divorce, which blocks the emotional impact of the separation. A physical analogy to this stage is the numbing shock that immediately follows a severe injury, in which the victim often feels nothing at all. Depression follows the initial emotional denial of the event in the case of both divorce and death, and then the recovery process starts, and the psyche—not without scars—can heal.

Death strikes most Americans with predictable weapons. *The New York Times* on February 4, 1976, reported that in 1974 heart disease was still the leading killer of Americans, and whereas fewer Americans were dying of strokes than in the past, more were dying of lung cancer. Most of these terminal illnesses gave some psychological or physical warning before they struck for the last time. In some cases, the victims had been seriously ill or noticeably disturbed in their minds for years before they died. The stress produced by serious sickness, not only in the victim himself, but in his family, is always severe. Until the early part of the twentieth century, families had to care for sick relatives at home, and the physical demands of carrying meals and baths, changing bed linen, and attending to the patients' wishes were arduous and often demanded time that could not be spared from the work the family had to do to support itself. However, doctors and psychologists who have studied the attitudes of critically ill people and their families now believe that having to care for the sick offers a way to exorcise a primeval, animallike hostility toward unwell fellow beings that lies buried in most people. Herds of reindeer or orangutans or zebras sometimes desert sick and dying members of the group because they cannot afford to slow their migrations in search of food to the pace of the sick. Primitive peoples—Australian aborigines and some African tribes—until recently followed similar patterns, and apparently the sense of being threatened by the ailing tribesman survives among us. Doctors who attend nursing homes report that when one member of an aged married couple becomes ill, often the other one is surprisingly eager to have his mate transferred to infirmary facilities and out of the room they share. In the photograph-and-text essay, *Gramp,* on an elderly man's last three years of life, there is a photograph of the aged and confused grandfather offering his wife a bouquet of weeds from the yard. She responded to his gesture as though he were still in his right mind and were deliberately taunting her. "Oh, Frank, if you really want to do something for me, why don't you clean this place up?" She had—in her late seventies—such a tenuous grasp on her own identity and health that she could not spare any tolerance for him.

Nursing homes and hospitals offer a ready receptacle for the sick whom their families are unconsciously eager to abandon but then often feel guilty about leaving, no matter how frightened or impatient they had been. It is, however, an unfortunate truth that for the nuclear family of today, living together in close quarters, to care for the aged and chronically ill would probably impose unbearable stress.

When caring for the sick is added to the stress imposed by poverty on a family who cannot afford hospital care and who may not be aware of public aid facilities, that family may disintegrate completely. Poverty is itself a source of unremitting stress that demands constant attention to the problem of survival and, consequently, leaves little time for attention to the well-being of a family unit. Although divorce is popularly considered to be a disease of the rich, in fact, divorce figures are much higher for lower-income groups. As with one old, sick person who cannot pity a sick spouse, giving emotionally to another may make too many demands when you are poor.

When illness attacks the children in a family, the feelings of parents and other family members are usually less ambivalent than they are toward older ailing relatives. In part because adults feel less threatened by the burden of sick children than they do by the incapacity of a spouse (their partner) or an aged parent (until then an authority figure), they are usually eager to give complete sympathy to their sick child. When they cannot cure the child or at least ease his discomfort, they feel, as many parents have attested, worse than if they themselves were in pain. Children are the objects of parents' immeasurable love, and that love contributes to the parent's sense of his own identity.

In fact, as long as we can focus on someone outside ourselves, we retain a unified self to look out from. The family bond that is manifested in a parent's feeling for a sick child can be felt as strongly by other family members. An old person who does *not* reject a sick mate and withdraw into the self sometimes places his whole life's purpose in the other person and keeps himself alive for him.

One piece of evidence of the strength of the human instinct for family ties is the fact that more than two-thirds of divorced Americans remarry within a short time after their divorces. Most divorced people, in fact, want to be married and have faith in family life—a faith which many writers have noted reflects Samuel Johnson's "triumph of hope over experience."

In whatever form family bonds manifest themselves, they are likely to be most satisfactory to the individual adult when he is giving from a position of strength, when he recognizes that he has responsibilities *both* to himself and to other people. Joseph Epstein quotes Hermann Keyserling, a German writer of the 1920s "what marriage is really about . . . is the acceptance of responsibility." Epstein continues:

> But if marriage is in the main about the acceptance of responsibility, and if, as Keyserling holds, "the essential difficulties of life begin with marriage," then why should anyone bother marrying in the first place? Because . . . marriage promotes self-development. Marriage is a relationship riddled with conflict—between self-interest and duty to one's partner and children, between personal ambition and social obligation, between the idea of marriage as a union of two people and the reality of both parties remaining at their core separate entities. It is because of these inherent conflicts that Keyserling called marriage a state of tragic tension. . . . "the fulfillment of marriage and its happiness entail the acceptance of the suffering pertaining to life. It gives the latter a new and deeper meaning. . . . *But whoever accepts suffering from the outset places himself in the very center of the meaning of life"* [author's italics].

The conclusion Epstein draws from Keyserling's remarks on marriage applies just as clearly to all family relationships. He says, "It was, then, in such terms that Count Keyserling saw marriage as a means of attaining the highest spiritual development of which men and women are capable."

Poverty and disease were often incurable until well into the twentieth century. (185) An immigrant mother, living in a cellar on New York's Lower East Side, was photographed in 1894 by Jacob Riis. The mother has bound her baby in traditional European swaddling clothes, but she seems doubtful that anything she does will be of any use against the damp, filth, and rats in her "home." The mattresses on which the family sleeps are rolled up behind her for the daytime. (186) Stress for families often lies in the uncertainty of how severe a given disruption may be. A New York City mother in 1953 tearfully hugged her daughter who had been lost during a summer holiday in Central Park. (187) Fear of the future, too, provokes family stress, whether it lasts for the minutes that tick by while a child is lost or whether it is chronic, as for this Ozark mother who waited in 1935 for another child to arrive, when she was not sure she could feed the ones she already had.

185

186

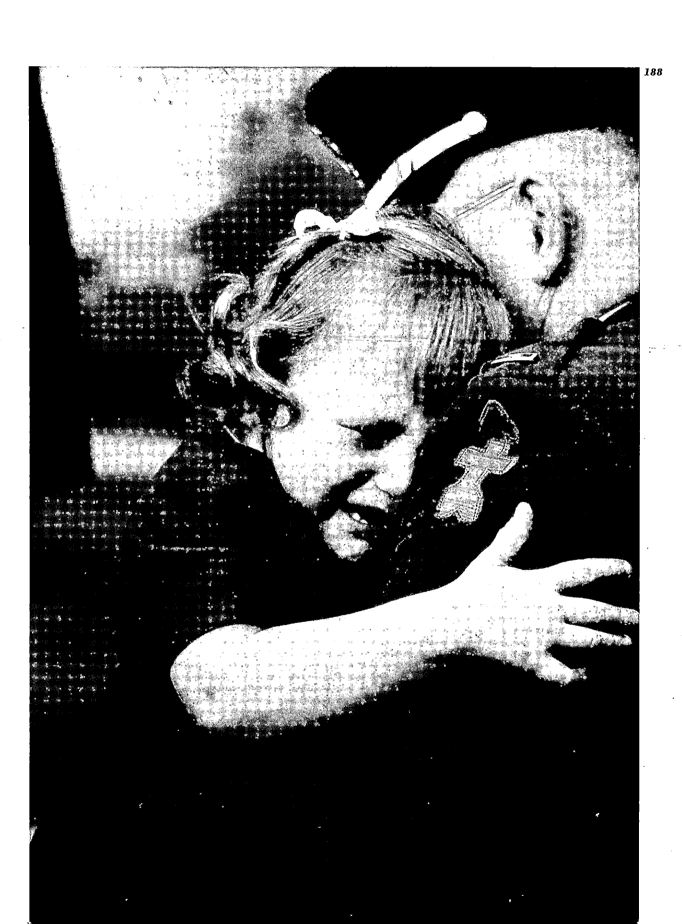

188

189

The suffering of families in wartime is quietly but movingly evoked in the photograph of
General Ord and his wife and daughter (1) in the first chapter of this book. (188) Here,
Pamela Farber, a small child in the 1960s, weeps bitterly when her father, an Army Reserve
officer, is called to active duty during the Berlin Wall crisis. (189) Mr. Farber returned home
unharmed, but even the threat of war suggests the possibility of a permanent division in the
family, as the face of a Wisconsin mother indicates. She was photographed when Reedsburg
reserve soldiers were called up in 1961. The call itself was destructive: soldiers had to give up
jobs and could not work their farms, and troubled marriages came apart during the
separation.

190

191

The dissolution of a marriage represents the collapse of one of the pillars of life. (190) *A Chicago man in 1948 rather histrionically expressed what the loss of his wife would mean by kneeling for the newspaper photographers outside the divorce court. She reconsidered.* (191) *High drama also characterized the case of the "Romantic Hoosier Plasterer," Howard Shaw, who was brought to court in 1939 by his fourth wife (left) on a swindle charge. His former fiancée (right) confirmed her story, saying he had extorted more than $10,000 from her, which he then spent on a honeymoon with the other woman. What saves the photograph and the situation from pure sensationalism is the set, tragic face of the fiancée.* (192) *The agony of children torn between parents who want nothing to do with each other lies in the split feelings the child must have. Here, after a custody case, a weeping child clings to the mother with whom she must leave, rejecting her father, who has not been awarded custody.*

192

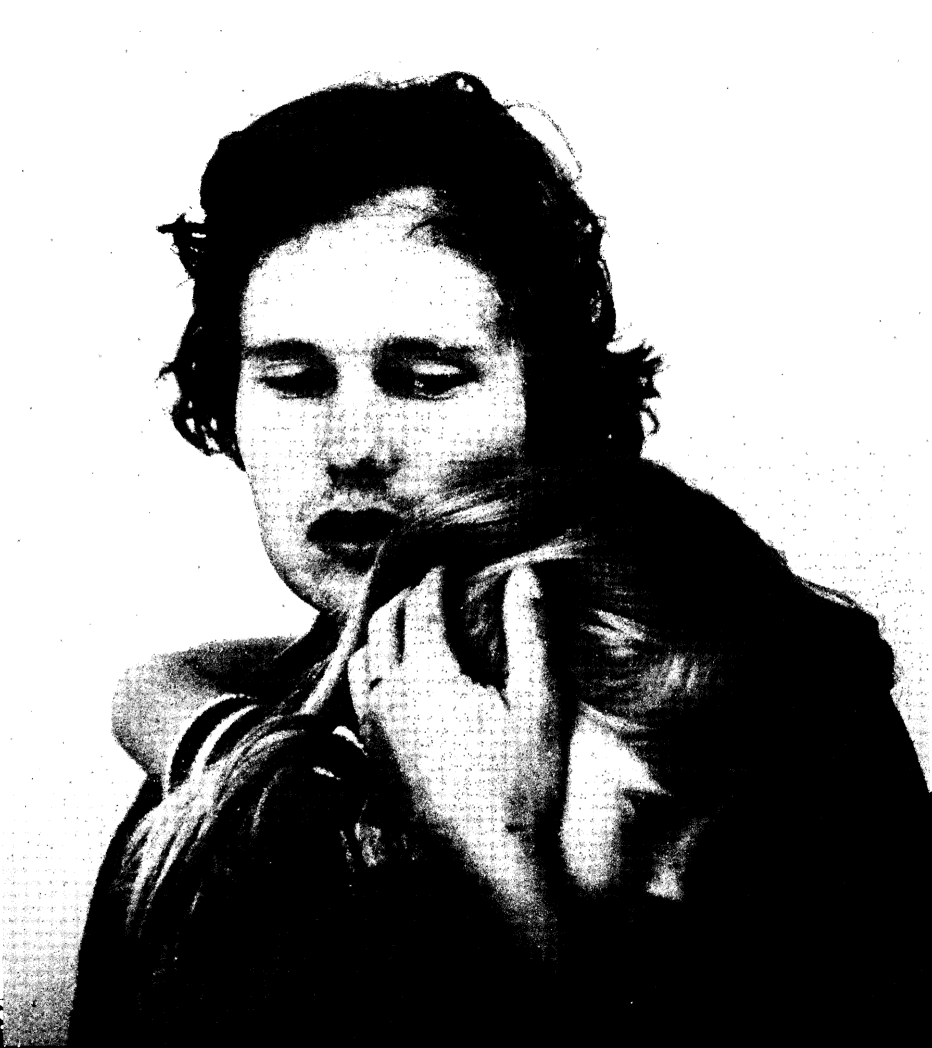

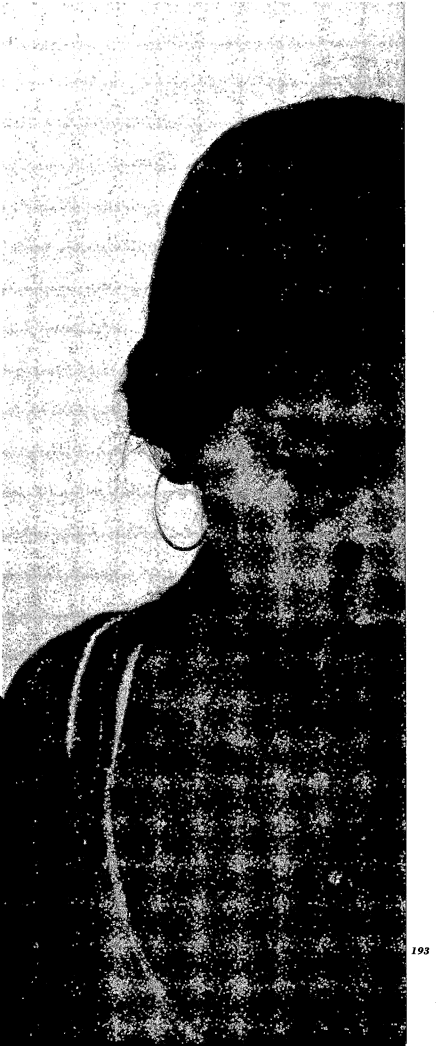

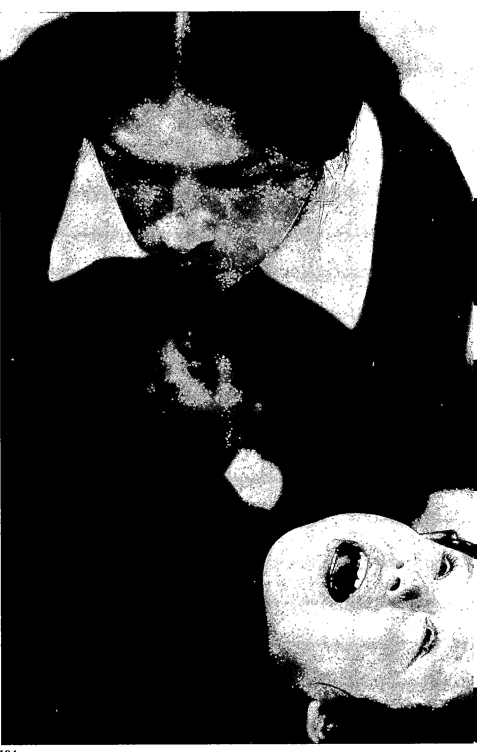

194

(193) *Feelings of stress and alienation pervade this photograph. A child clings to her pensive father, while the mother looks in another direction, remote in her own thoughts.* (194) *The pain that is all the greater because a loved one bears it is reflected on this California mother's taut face as her child, undergoing bone-marrow aspiration, shrieks at the insertion of a hypodermic needle through his spine.*

193

195

(195) *Coming from her husband's sick room, an elderly Vermont woman meets her son on the stairs.* (196) *Dan Jury closes the eyes of his grandfather, a Pennsylvania coal miner, whom the family tended at home during the three years of his decline and final illness. "Gramp's" daughter weeps in the background. Now that the burden of care has been abruptly lifted, the family may find themselves disoriented and floating without direction.*

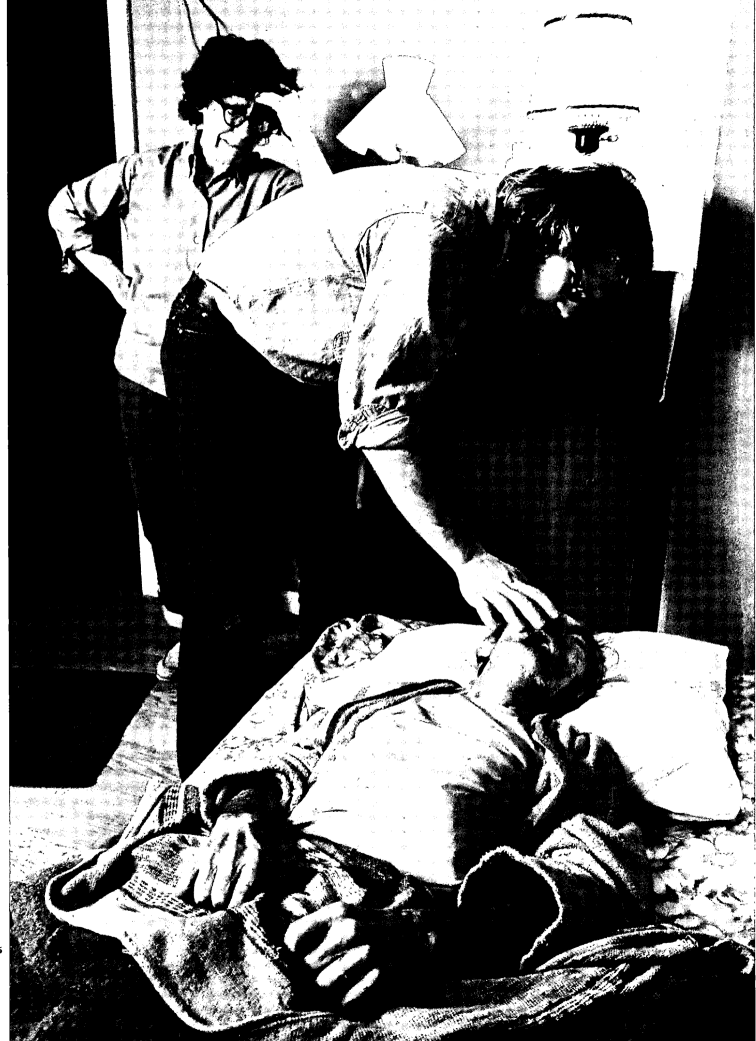

Holidays

The American domestic year is like a seesaw, nicely balanced by the two most important holidays. At one end is Christmas with its cold weather, loads of presents, families gathering to bicker and love, the magic of Santa Claus for children, and deep religious meaning. Press down the other end and there is the Fourth of July, sitting brown and smiling in the bright glare of summer, bringing picnics, beer, swimming, and broiling car trips and decked with firecrackers and flags that are as vestigial in their modern context as the manger often is to Christmas. Encompassing in the same observance a private celebration, on the one hand, and a public and commercial display, on the other, has characterized these American holidays since their inception.

The Puritans distrusted the Christmas festivity as it had evolved in Elizabethan England because they felt that public celebration had overwhelmed the significance of Christ's birth. In Massachusetts, Christmas was ignored altogether; Judge Samuel Sewall noted in his diary of 1686, "Some somehow observe the day [Christmas], but are vexed, I believe, that the body of the People profane [do not celebrate] it, and blessed be God no authority yet to compell them to keep it." In a sense, this fuss about Christmas was illogical because the Puritans turned around and decreed their own state holiday of Thanksgiving, which had, of course, a religious significance. They felt, however, that Thanksgiving was properly a public holiday because its purpose was to thank God for the survival of the whole community. Besides, the Puritans were always sure that their community—i.e., their state—was in covenant with God. Whatever the Puritan state did had religious implications because it was composed of religious individuals, and the individual was held responsible for the actions of the state and his fellow citizens. In fact, periodically, public fast days were declared, when the whole community went to the meetinghouse and spent the day in fasting and prayer to atone for the state's errors. A fast of repentance was ordered for January 14, 1697, to express remorse for the gruesome mistake of the Salem witchcraft trials. Another such fast-day proclamation declared, "Some English, by selling strong *Drink* unto *Indians* have not only prejudiced the Designs of Christianitie but also been the Faulty and Bloody occasions of Death, among them . . . Thursday [shall] bee kept as a Day of *Humiliation* by prayer with *Fasting.* "

Because these holidays (in the old sense of the word, they were solemn "holy days") came out of the community's concerns, celebrating them bound the community together. It is the individual's experience of setting aside a day—whether in humiliation or joy—and spending it in communion with his fellows—family members, church members, citizens—that gives a holiday its meaning. The holiday is meaningful to the individual himself and because others are like him, to the community as a whole. This is why Christmas is important to each Christian and to the church as a whole, why the Fourth of July is important to each citizen and to the nation as a whole, and why Yom Kippur is important to each Jew and to the Jewish people as a whole.

In the family, the smallest social unit of the community, the sense of festivity that flows between the individual and the group is particularly strong. For a child, each holiday is full of wonder and mystery in its transcendence of the customary because the adult pillars of the child's world are atremble with excitement themselves. Hannah Green's memoir *The Dead of the House* suggests what such a family ritual as the lighting of a Christmas tree can mean.

> When, at six-thirty, we came downstairs, Daddy had lighted the coal fire in the grate. The lamps
> were on and soft, the curtains drawn, and just as we came into the living room Daddy lighted the

(197) *The Christmas tree has been a feature of American celebration for well over one hundred years. This turn-of-the-century tree combines traditional popcorn strings with new patent ornaments such as the fashionable angel on top. In 1880 Woolworth's bought $25 worth of Christmas-tree ornaments from a supplier; a few years later, the order had risen to $800,000.*

tree. And there it was on the night before Christmas, the branches reaching out and up, and in the spaces between there seemed to be a spirit caught. The branches were wound round and hung with lights and angel's hair and candy canes and colored balls, which were like myriad mirrors reflecting tiny living rooms and the tiny, funny faces of us as we drew close. Amy was soft-footed and enchanted, looking up.

The child, self-centered as are all the very young, feels sure somehow that it's all for him. This is probably the first sense of holiday we have, and it is the one that sticks with us. Our early memory of the family doing something grand seemingly just for us—of the community celebrating together in our behalf—is perhaps what leads many adults who have no family to say they hate Christmas—or hate holidays in general. Not only is their lack of family emphasized, but they feel out of step with their whole national or racial culture. It is un-American to dislike Christmas! Or, you are not a good Jew if you don't celebrate Passover. It is through our first family ties that holidays are significant; those allegiances lead to community ties. Somehow at holiday time, if family ties are lacking, it is almost as though our community ties themselves had dissolved.

In the interest of community traditions, New Englanders continued to discourage any special notice of December 25 well into the nineteenth century. In much of the Northeast, Christmas was just acknowledged by a family dinner. A historian of Christmas customs, Phillip Snyder, has indicated that, as late as 1855, banks, stores, and even courtrooms functioned in New York City on December 25, just as on any other business day. But Snyder has researched a *New York Times* article for December 26,1855, which indicates celebrating Christmas was a well-established custom in New York's German community. The *Times* somewhat smugly observed: "We always pity Yankees on the 25th of December. They scarcely know what the day means, and, strange as it may seem, they are almost equally ignorant of the proper way to spend New-Year's." This display of ignorance was especially shocking to the New Yorkers who had inherited the old Dutch custom of keeping Christmas as an exclusively religious holiday and observing New Year's Day with calls and merriment and wine punch. Many fashionable city dwellers by the 1880s, in fact, observed New Year's so enthusiastically—some made as many as forty calls in one day with a glass of punch at each house—that the holiday was deplored by the soberer citizenry as a tipsy excuse for letting down all barriers, much as New Year's Eve is regarded nowadays.

An overflowing table can add to the sense of family communion when everyone enjoys a huge Christmas meal together. Paul Engle, in the *American Heritage* issue of December 1957, remembered the wondrous dinners that were given by his family at their Iowa farm in the early decades of the century.

There are no dinners like that anymore: every item from the farm itself, with no deep freezer, no car for driving into town for packaged food. The pies had been baked the day before, pumpkin, apple and mince; as we ate them, we could look out the window and see the cornfield where the pumpkins grew, the trees from which the apples were picked. There was cottage cheese, with the dripping bags of curds still hanging from the cold cellar ceiling. The bread had been baked that morning, heating up the oven for the meat, and as my aunt hurried by I could smell in her apron that freshest of all odors with which the human nose is honored—bread straight from the oven. There would be a huge crock of beans with smoked pork from the hog butchered every November. We could see, beyond the crock, the broad black iron kettle in a corner of the barnyard, turned upside down, the innocent hogs stopping to scratch on it. There would be every form of preserve: wild grape from the vines in the grove, crab apple jelly, wild blackberry and tame raspberry, strawberry from the bed in the garden, sweet and sour pickles with dill from the edge of the lane where it grew wild, pickles from the rind of the same watermelon we had cooled in the tank at the milk house and eaten on a hot September afternoon.

The abundance that makes Christmas so festive is often transferred away from the products that the family has grown or produced to what they can buy. The present-giving aspect of Christmas, so flamboyantly evident today, has been denounced as regularly as the Puritans denounced the festive English Christmas. Indeed, commercialism seems to have taken over, and young families go into debt and deprive themselves all year so that their Christmas-club bank account will be fat enough. Emphasis on presents seemed to increase with the new ready money that industry provided after the Civil War. R.H. Macy's remained open for the first time on Christmas Eve in 1867 and did a whopping (for those days) six-thousand-dollars-worth of business that day. One third of the nation's new books were sold in the six weeks before Christmas in 1910, and, by 1950, one quarter of the jewelry sold during the year was bought in December. Christmas catalogues from such expensive stores as Neiman-Marcus in Dallas have offered in the recent past "His and Her jaguars"—a car for Him for $5,559, a coat for Her for $5,975; or you may select a Jewel-of-the-Month—each month during the New Year the store will deliver a different piece of jewelry for a mere $273,950. Tiffany's, one year, offered Flora Danica dessert plates at $1000 per dozen, and Abercrombie and Fitch outdid them with a hand-tooled backgammon set for $1000 for just the one set.

But looking beyond such grotesque excess and the frantic accumulation, one realizes that children's very real sense of the miraculous at Christmas is distinctly fostered by present-giving. Children are pragmatic and usually immediate in their desires; and for small children who are hedged about by great creatures laying down rules that seem arbitrary and sometimes downright whimsical, how perfect must a day be in which all wishes are granted and most anger and rules are suspended. Classicist Robert Fitzgerald's memoir of his father that appeared in *The New Yorker* magazine in 1976 indicates how Santa Claus and presents can bring a child to find a deeper meaning in Christmas.

> [Father] is attentive to the children's observances of Easter and Christmas, as well as the Fourth of July. The life of Santa Claus we learn from him in such elaborate detail that it will be years before the reindeer disappear from the winter sky. One Christmas Eve they become actually visible, jingling down the street between the snowdrifts to stop and toss their antlers in the starlight in front of our house. Then, sure enough, we see a portly figure get out of the sleigh, and we are so excited we can no longer bear to stay at the window; there is a thunderclap of laughter at the door, and Santa Claus in scarlet and white tosses a great armload of small packages and nuts and oranges into the room. I wonder if that apparition, staged with such professional art, predisposed me to faith in the mythical and the magical.

In the West, in pioneer times, oranges were a great delicacy and seldom seen. Many a child of the frontier got only a home-knitted muffler for Christmas and an orange, lodged like a small cannonball in the toe of his Christmas stocking, but those wonderful spheres, appearing from nowhere, produced just as much sense of the mythical and the magical as the fastest self-propelling scooter that F.A.O. Schwarz ever devised.

The stockings in which presents were stuffed began to be edged out in importance by Christmas trees on which presents were hung in the late nineteenth century; one *New York Times* writer, correctly assessed as a "curmudgeon" by scholar Phillip Snyder, feared that the trees struck a blow at the very essence of Christmas. "The German Christmas tree—a rootless and lifeless corpse—was never worthy of the day, and no one can say how far the spirit of rationalism, which begins with the denial of Santa Claus, the supernatural filler of stockings, and ends with the denial of all things supernatural, has been fostered by the German Christmas trees, which have been so widely adopted in this country."

But the sense of the "supernatural" survived and even benefited from the introduction of the Christmas trees; in fact, American holidays have always benefited from an infusion of immigrant blood. The first Christmas trees, mentioned in a *Saturday Evening Post* article in 1825 as twinkling through the windows of the houses of Philadelphia, were brought there by the Pennsylvania Germans years before Queen Victoria's Prince Albert introduced them to England in the 1840s. Other contributions of the Pennsylvania Germans were Easter eggs and the Easter bunny. An early Christain symbol of the resurrection of Christ (because from the hard tomb of the egg comes new life), eggs were particularly popular as a symbol of spring, as well, as in the folk cultures of Germany and Eastern Europe, where winter held the land in a rocklike grip until the ice cracked and the new life of the year appeared. The origin of the rabbit as a symbol of springtime or new life is more obscure, but perhaps it is related to the rabbit's notable fecundity. In any case, nineteenth-century Pennsylvania-German housewives baked large rabbits out of cookie dough and depicted them in the act of laying a cookie-dough egg. Although the idea was biologically unsound, the miraculous bunny delighted children until Victorian sensibility decreed that the birth process, even fancifully presented, was not a suitable family topic.

221

If the various ethnic groups have added a dash of foreign spice to our melting pot of holidays, the impact of American life on the celebration of those foreign holidays transplanted here has often been unhappy for immigrant families in transition. For many new immigrants to the United States in the latter part of the nineteenth century, holidays were an all-important means of maintaining their ethnic identity. In the case of the Jews, holidays had affirmed that identity through centuries of civil persecution. For Catholic peoples like the Italians and the Irish, the saint's-day feasts—San Gennaro, San Antonio, Saint Patrick—strengthened ties with the old way of life, in which the great festivals had played an important role, punctuating the monotony of the peasant's round—flowers bursting into bloom in the arid soil of drudgery that constituted daily life.

When the second-generation immigrant moved out of the communal life of the ghetto and into the American business community, holidays became a source of family pain and conflict. For the parents, the holiday was a familiar and comforting landmark in what remained a strange existence; for the children, the holiday was at once a point of communication with their parents and a brake holding them back from new lives. *The New York Tribune* reported on September 30, 1900:

> [The second generation Jew] learns to surrender his celebration of other religious days for business reasons. Thus, little by little, the Jewish boy is transformed into a workaday member of the American business community. Natural as such a result is, it brings with it endless unhappiness to Jewish homes on the East Side. The father, with bewildered sorrow, sees his child steadily becoming estranged from him, not merely in education and the ordinary things of American life, but even in the observance of rites and laws peculiar to his race through countless centuries.

Holidays that were meant to cement family relations and affirm a racial identity underwent severe transplant shock when they were shifted to New World soil and often proved more divisive than unifying. Frequently, the third generation wanted to find its roots again and would revive the old holiday observances, but until there was leisure and emotional distance for such tender remembrance, the immigrant experience of holidays could be blighting.

Having no national holidays on which to pin its own sense of nationhood, the United States set out in the early nineteenth century to create some and hasn't stopped since. Historian Daniel Boorstin has assembled a list of holidays currently observed in America. Somebody here celebrates somewhere, at some time, Arbor Day, Fast Day, Robert E. Lee's Birthday, Lincoln's Birthday, Texas Independence Day, Bunker Hill Day, Columbus Day, Nathan Bedford Forrest's Birthday, Andrew Jackson's Birthday, Thomas Jefferson's Birthday, Bennington Battle Day, Huey P. Long's Birthday, Pulaski Day, Confederate Memorial Day, Will Rogers Day, Flag Day, and many more. All of these probably mean about as much to the ordinary American family as Washington's Birthday, which is acknowledged merely by the closing of banks and the appearance in bakery windows of cakes decorated with cherries and little hatchets. The relatively feeble hold of such holidays on people's hearts—where their sense of tradition lives—is attested to by the fact that the observance of Lincoln's and Washington's birthdays has recently been shifted to a long weekend midway between the actual dates, and no one has objected. When, in 1939, Franklin Delano Roosevelt attempted to move Thanksgiving from the traditional last Thursday in November to the fourth Thursday, there was such confusion and outcry that some communities celebrated twice, on successive Thursdays. Perhaps the American people are simply more flexible now, but it may also be inferred that the more meaningful a holiday is, the less likely people are to permit its being tampered with. Very rarely is a newly declared holiday immediately and profoundly meaningful to large numbers of people, but Martin Luther King Day, commemorating the great civil-rights leader's death and recognizing, all too belatedly, the black contribution to American life, has become part of the American cultural fabric in a few years' time.

The Fourth of July, our principal national holiday, is important in the lives of families, if only because it usually becomes an excuse to make a long summer weekend. But, beyond that, no one is quite sure why it is important. It isn't really even a date when anything happened, nineteenth-century rhetoric and modern Broadway musicals to the contrary. It was on July 2, not July 4, that the Continental Congress voted to accept the resolution that "these United Colonies are, and of right ought to be, free and independent States."

How July 4 eventually became accepted as the date of the birth of the American nation casts interesting light on the way holidays achieve their hold. Around the beginning of the nineteenth century, the Fourth of July was not much of a holiday at all. It had been appropriated by both the Federalist party of John

Adams and the Republican party of Thomas Jefferson, and, when one party was in political power and staged a celebration, the other party would not participate. A newspaper in Vincennes, Indiana, said in the early nineteenth century, "Since office seekers and demagogues often monopolize the proceedings [on the Fourth], it is undignified to share in them." Then, on July 4, 1826, both Thomas Jefferson and John Adams died. This coincidence, occurring, moreover, on the fiftieth anniversary of independence, seemed a supernatural sign that the day was consecrated. A touch of mystery set the day apart, and from that jubilee year the Fourth was felt to be truly our birthday.

The way the Fourth was celebrated, as more legends and sentiment accrued to it, remained fairly simple. There was usually a parade, and, until they were safely and boringly put under civic control in the mid-twentieth century, there were firecrackers at home, and in the streets. For small boys, from the time of the Civil War until World War II, firecrackers—those symbolic guns of a revolution long sunk into peace and prosperity—made the day dangerously unique. Children saved their money for weeks to buy pinwheels, and Roman candles, and even the giant fireworks that lit up to display the flag against the night sky in fire. Homemade firecrackers were the worst, as Lucretia Hales's comic novel of the 1870s, *The Peterkin Papers,* ruefully remembers: "Mrs. Peterkin had always been afraid of fireworks, and had never allowed the boys to bring gunpowder into the house. She was even afraid of torpedoes; they looked so much like sugarplums she was sure some of the children would swallow them, and explode before anybody knew it." One fiendishly simple firecracker prescription called for gunpowder and a tin can; you put the one under the other, attached a fuse, lit it, and waited for the can to be blown literally sky-high. Sometimes, if the can didn't go up when it should, foolhardy boys bent over it to see what was wrong and lost an eye.

But the danger, the family arguments over whether little Josiah or Chauncey or Ned should be allowed to buy firecrackers this year, and the fun of choosing from a kaleidoscopic array of wheels, crackers, serpents, flowerpots, sparklers, and rockets made the day memorable and noisy, and nearly as exciting as Christmas. And what was more important, it made the day special for each family. Speeches in the park were long, but the plentitude of picnics made up for them. What had been the date when a group of sweating men in wigs and short pants met and argued and voted, the supposed birthday of a concept spawned by eighteenth-century philosophers and economics and producing a nation, became, in the hearts and memories of millions, their very own special day when work stopped and fried chicken was eaten and everybody was together at home.

198

199

200

The advent of spring has coincided with the celebration of Easter and the Jewish Passover festival for centuries. Easter was regarded with disfavor by the Puritans as a papist celebration, but the holiday endured and became festive after the Civil War, with Easter parades and Easter-egg hunts. (198) Members of Chicago's prosperous black community stand outside church on Easter Sunday in 1941. Everyone wears the smartest of new clothes, and little sister hugs the bunny she could not be induced to leave at home. (199) President Rutherford B. Hayes inaugurated the Easter-egg roll on the White House lawn in 1878, and, despite the risk to the carpet, similar rolls took place in parlors across the land. These children, about 1905, were surrounded by eggs and lilies. The blossom growing from the bulb and the new life in the egg are symbols both of Christ's emergence from the tomb and of the earth's new life in springtime. (200) The solemn but joyous Passover celebration has retained the essential components of wine, bitter herbs, and unleavened bread since the Israelites assembled these staples for their flight from Egypt three thousand years ago.

203

From the Civil War to World War I, Independence Day was as much a community holiday as
Christmas was a private family celebration. (201) Children in Kingsfield, Maine, in the 1890s
assembled their own small parade, heralding the glorious Fourth with horns and
flags. (202) A Sunday-school class at the turn of the century parades proudly with its
banner past a reviewing stand draped with bunting on Independence Day in Central
Park. (203) Today, with firecrackers outlawed and speechifying in disrepute, the Fourth is
more likely to be observed by a barbecue with family and neighbors. This storm-fenced
backyard is in the New York City borough of Queens, but it could be any place in the nation.

Thanksgiving, a celebration of plenty—in its earliest days, of sufficiency—has changed less in character than any other holiday. First declared a national holiday in 1863 by President Lincoln, Thanksgiving has centered around turkey and all the trimmings from its New England inception. (206) This turn-of-the-century family enjoyed a diverse menu that may have included fried oysters and venison pasty with their bird. (207, 208) The Earle Landis family of Neffsville, Pennsylvania, concentrated on the business of eating after thanks were returned. The Landises were photographed during World War II by Farm Security Administration photographers who were directed to record our prosperity for morale purposes.

206

207

208

205

Old pagan holidays that the Puritans had left behind in England were dusted off in the late nineteenth century as celebrations for children. (204) May Day did not enjoy a long revival, but at its peak of popularity, around 1900, girls in white dresses made a pretty sight dancing with colored ribbons around a maypole and leaving May baskets of flowers on doorsteps. (205) Halloween, brought to America by the Irish, who delighted in its superstitious rites, was an occasion for fortune-telling and games from the 1880s on. Trick-or-treat was a twentieth-century elaboration: The excitement of little masked figures scurrying around the neighborhood is suggested here.

209

(209, 210) *The Christmas pageant at church is many a child's first terror-stricken public appearance as a performer; once the excitement is over, the sense of Christmas as a festival that unites whole congregations and communities stays with the child during the family tree-trimming and present-opening at home.*

Rites of Passage

Small-town business districts around the turn of the century used to regularly witness a scene that everybody recognized as an important turning point in the life of a boy. In fact, it was a rite of passage, although most of the people watching wouldn't have called it that. A matron, probably wearing an elaborate hat, with her long skirts trailing on the board or brick sidewalk, would come decidedly down the street followed by a boy of fourteen or so who wore a cap, jacket, and the knee-length trousers called knickerbockers—or more commonly just "knickers." The pair would turn into one of the stores and disappear into its dark interior; when they emerged, twenty minutes or so later, the boy, no longer ambling carelessly behind his mother, stood straighter, walked with a swagger, and attempted with great *savior faire* to suppress a grin—and all because he wore a pair of long pants. All of his friends could see those trouser bottoms touching his boots and know that he was a man. An African boy has soot rubbed into open cuts to make a ritual tattoo, an Indian boy has to bring back his first game alone; for more than fifty years in America, donning long pants was the rite of passage that signaled to the community and a youth's peer group that he had left childhood behind. On one side of the trouser-buying bridge, little boys played jacks and mumblety-peg and rolled hoops; on the other side, free and independent citizens of the world's most glorious republic smoked cigars, fought Indians, and, with discretion, even imbibed liquor (or so the new land of adulthood appeared at the crucial moment of arrival).

This type of rite of passage that marked an individual's coming of age as an adult member of the community is the most ancient kind of rite. And it is, significantly, the peer group and the community as a whole that such rites are meant to impress. The family, really, is not involved except in implementing the child's departure from their care for his own place in the world. Although the family had to finance and condone the purchase of the long pants, at home it made little difference whether Junior wore knickers, long pants, or dresses. It was the approval of the community that was to be won by the young person's adoption of its mores.

The reason that most rites of passage celebrate some involvement of an individual in society rather than interaction among family members has been suggested by Philippe Ariès in his seminal study of attitudes about the family, *Centuries of Childhood*. Ariès theorizes that until the seventeenth century, when the increased prosperity of the bourgeoisie made such deliberately organized social units as nations, cities, and *families* important for the stability of trade, the family as a social unit did not count for very much. Instead of living strictly in families, people in the Middle Ages and early Renaissance also lived in natural groups that resulted from early patterns of defense or, simply, proximity: Clans clustered together, castles sheltered lords and vassals of all ranks, village huts huddled against each other for protection against marauders roaming the open fields. In that world, "family" meant the ancestry and bloodline of the nobility; members of ordinary families kept themselves distinct from the community only for the most basic purposes of sex or birth or nursing. Domestically, you lived, literally, with your neighbors; the rooms in castles and big houses all opened out of each other and no room in which people lived was designated for any particular purpose—many people ate and slept in each room. This is not true in modern times, when the family detaches itself and provides identity for its members. In the Middle Ages, man identified himself as a peasant or a cobbler or a youth or an old codger before he would conceive himself as belonging to a certain family.

(211) *One's passage through life is as likely to be marked by members of the community as by the family; these Lawrence, Kansas, youngsters got an early start at a baby birthday party in 1900, where everyone was photographed ranged around a glumly crowned birthday child.*

Many rites that we celebrate today are survivals of early ones in which a person was welcomed or initiated into a social class or age group or profession, rather than into some kind or stage of family relationship. The very first rites of passage experienced by children other than birthdays are of very ancient origin—medieval or earlier—for they denote the passage of the child into membership in a religious faith. Christening or baptism, first communion for Roman Catholics, and the Bar Mitzvah ceremony for Jewish boys at puberty all celebrate the union of a young soul with the great body of the faith. The family is enjoined to nurture the faith as they nurture the child, but the focus is on the overarching, eternal religious institution and on the child's standing as an individual within it, just as in the Middle Ages, when one's connection to the community of church and castle was one's primary identity.

Birthdays, though they resemble medieval rites in that they mark the individual's progress through the world, are the product of the post-Renaissance (and therefore "modern") attitude that stable social units and precision about measurements of money, distance, and time are important. In the medieval world there were no birthdays. Records were imprecise, illiteracy was general, and age, except as it affected how well you could perform, didn't really matter. As a result, people often didn't know or bother to remember when they were born. Birthdays became significant when other measurements and units of order became necessary to insure the peaceful flow of trade. Thomas Cromwell, Henry VIII of England's opportunistic government minister, first decreed in 1538 that every citizen had to know and register the date of his birth. Cromwell was one of the founders of the strong, centrally governed modern nation as we know it, and it is significant that he stressed the importance of birthdays, which are part of the system of guy-wires tieing the modern citizen to his particular place in the state.

Birthdays are celebrated regularly by families, as well as noted by the state, but they really record in an eerie way a person's lone wanderings through life. Birthdays have borrowed one of the most ancient symbols of ritual and church, the candle, as their symbol. The life of fire—and, by extension, all life—that candles quite literally embody in their flickering is all too realistically snuffed out as the birthday celebrant draws his breath and blows out the years. The strong grip that rites of passage have on our imaginations is nowhere better demonstrated than in the primitive response of middle-aged people who refuse to celebrate birthdays, feeling somehow that if they don't recognize the rite, no forward movement has been made and they can't be any older.

Many of the informal (or perhaps one should say unofficial, since rites of passage are rarely without form) markers of a child's progression in life emphasize his movement away from the family and into the community. The first tricycle, little boys' loss of long curls in Victorian times, little girls' gradually lengthening skirts at the same period, a boy's first razor, all denote the child's growing independence of the family. The tyranny of community and peer group generally overrides all family authority in the matter of when such rites should occur. It is a strong-minded parent who can resist the plea that "everyone is doing it", and today, when the strength of the adolescent sub-culture reinforces traditional community pressure to absorb the young person into itself, families have a hard time postponing social rites.

The rites a young person must encounter within the peer group are elaborate and precise. Sexual initiation, codified in parts of Europe for boys with a visit to a brothel, has always been covert but sought after, too, in America. There is a prescribed set of jokes and hints among boys suggesting sexual experience and prowess. (A friend of the author tells of his high-school basketball team in the early 1960s, every member of which would be sure to drop his wallet in the locker room so that his teammates could see the outline of the prophylactic kept therein—the implication being that the wallet's owner was so sexually active he couldn't afford to be unequipped for a minute.) Mysterious silences and pullings-aside of confidential friends among girls communicate the same message to the group. Then, for both, a kind of mating dance takes place; in small towns, boys drive in one direction around the square and girls in the other until somebody stops and offers an elaborately casual invitation. Different signs indicate different stages of social and sexual maturity until the harassed young adult who has kept his footing on the stepping-stones of high-school and college waters gains the far bank, where he will supposedly be a "free" adult.

When such a young adult has gone through all the rites liberating him from the family, then he finds one day that he is about to undergo the final rite of the full-fledged adult and adopt anew the burden he cast off

and burrow back into the family.

Weddings were not particularly important until the family unit became an important social unit in the seventeenth century. Before that, the marriage contract was looked on as a way of preserving and transferring property and propagating the race. Saint Paul's sour strictures had early biased the Christian religion against marriage as anything more than a social necessity, and it was the social—not the religious—character of weddings that stood out. Sociologist Edward Shorter says, "It was at weddings . . . that the community thrust itself most forcefully into the 'vital' elements of personal life. . . . in traditional Europe the wedding was open on all sides." When the couple came out of church, the young people of a village would demand forfeits of drink and food or they would harass the wedding party. This public, social character of weddings was characteristic of early American practices, too. Puritan magistrates married Massachusetts Bay Colony couples in the meetinghouse—which was emphatically only a building for meetings of all sorts, not a church consecrated to religious celebration—or, more frequently, couples were married in front of the parlor fireplace at home. There was usually a feast for most of the community, even in New England, and in the back-country South for most of the eighteenth and nineteenth centuries there survived a raucous European peasant custom known as shivaree. This jolly extension of the wedding festivities called for young men of the community to sneak under the windows of the room where the newly married couple were spending their first night and serenade them with catcalls and by banging on washtubs and gongs and shooting their guns into the air. A colonial version of the European *charivari,* which subjected erring members of the community to public humiliation, the shivaree was a pointed demonstration of the fact that the community did not intend to lose the newlyweds in any private paradise of their own domesticity. At the presumably most intimate moment of their lives, the young couple were audibly reminded that they were still members of the community.

Before the Civil War, most weddings took place in the home of the bride and were primarily events for the whole community to take part it. But winds were shifting as the family became more important—indeed, more important than the community for many mobile Americans. An author of an etiquette book in the 1850s, deploring former wedding customs, revealed just how much of a community function the event had been.

> We hope and believe that the frolics which were once customary at weddings, have become obsolete—the deep and riotous drinking, from which the bridegroom had to be carried to bed; the games and jests, often indecent; the general kissing of the bride, a distasteful and even disgusting practice; the ceremonies of bedding the couple, which may have been all well enough in the "good old times" we read about, but which are utterly inconsistent with our present ideas of refinement.

"Our present ideas of refinement" tended to be, in fact, notions of ostentation, indulged in as far as the bridal family's purse would allow, because, significantly, as the family itself became a stronger institution apart from the community, the public display the family put on seemed to increase. It was almost as though the family unit was seeking to compensate for its withdrawal from participation in the community by putting a showy image in its place, the way an African doctor might leave an elaborate doll in his shrine to satisfy supplicants while he himself is active elsewhere. As the community was increasingly excluded from active participation in the wedding, the public character of the ceremony had to be shown all the more emphatically. The elaborate trappings of contemporary weddings were nearly all present by the 1880s. Ranks of ushers and bridesmaids, banks of flowers, mountains of food, legions of relatives, and tables groaning under presents in duplicate and triplicate distinguished turn-of-the-century weddings as they do modern ones. The cost was proportionally as disproportionate to the family's income then as now.

The wedding anniversaries that are celebrated by the immediate participants every year and by other members of the family and friends at intervals of ten or twenty-five or fifty years afterward do finally achieve the status of family rites of passage. The occasion enables the family to celebrate its own continuity through change, and the feeling at anniversaries can be quite intense. Many people are concentrating on the continuity of a social group that is small enough to have a great deal of meaning for almost everyone involved.

The final rite for an individual, marking his ultimate passage from life to death, is, of course, his funeral, and it is here that the family often makes the most determined effort to establish the continuity that exists through change. In colonial America, when the neighbors attended a funeral, each person was given a pair of black gloves, a black scarf, and a mourning ring to unify their observance and make a community of the mourners themselves. Judge Samuel Sewall, that articulate old Puritan, noted in his diary regarding an acquaintance's burial: "I was not at his Funeral. Had Gloves sent me, but the knowledge of his notoriously wicked life made me sick of going . . . and so I staid at home, and by that means lost a Ring." On the frontier, funerals were the means of asserting the existence of a community that was little more than incipient and drawing them together from scattered clearings for the comfort of the bereaved family. One personal historian of Ohio's frontier days remembers that

> when anyone died, a boy was sent on horseback from house to house to tell the sad tidings. On the day of the funeral, all the men and women in the country round laid aside their work, however important, and attended it. Rough wagons, with boards across for seats, perhaps with a chair for some old grandmother, formed the procession, followed often by men on horseback with their wives behind them. They had no hearse and the best wagon of the settlement held the coffin, and a homespun blanket answered for a pall. . . . I have never seen anything that seemed to me so solemn as those wagons winding through the forests and over rough roads to the half-cleared graveyard of that new country.

From being genuine community events, centered on the family (bodies were washed and dressed for burial at home, and the funeral service was usually held there, too), funerals, like weddings, evolved in the twentieth century into private rites with many expensive trappings displayed to notify and, at the same time, fend off the community. In 1960 Americans spent $1.6 billion on funerals—more than they spent on higher education in the same year. These terribly expensive modern funerals that can cost up to $2500 for an ordinary middle-class one have been removed from ordinary public ritual sites and transported to the perfumed back rooms of funeral parlors. Undertakers began to direct funerals (and thus became "funeral directors") around the turn of the century. They had emerged from the ranks of small-town businessmen in a very logical way: Some were livery-stable keepers—who had the horses needed to pull a hearse—or furniture-store owners—who had the lumber and varnish and upholstery needed for a coffin—or church sextons—who had charge of the graveyard. Today, embalming a corpse and "undertaking" its funeral is a major American business in its own right, but it does not necessarily make the solemnity of the ritual commensurate with the expense, although that is what is supposed to happen. In fact, as with many other rites in modern America, funerals have been taken away from the community and made available as anonymous services to be bought and paid for by the isolated nuclear family.

Rites of passage mark the movement of the individual out of and into society at different times in his life. What they also mark, inexorably, is the passage of time. In this, they are connected permanently to the family because the family is the strongest agency we have that seems to retard time's passing. In the Middle Ages, time was not as important as the cycles of the seasons; a man was born, in due season he was wed, in due season he was laid to rest. There was little other concern with time, and the great institutions of church and nobility seemed as immutable as the ever-visible cathedral and castle looming above the plain where the peasant tilled the soil. It was enough to belong to communities; they were there in all seasons. When people began to move to the towns, however, there were suddenly more opportunities. Life stretched out like a road. With the discovery of America and the manifold changes of technology in succeeding centuries, what might happen on the road of life could be infinitely varied, and on this road one was alone. Companions fell away and new ones joined the trek but it was alone that one spent a good part of the journey. The companions you could count on for company for the longest period of the trip were the family you started with or married into and helped create. The community continually changed, but the family remained. They saw you move from Sloughs of Despond to Delectable Mountains and because they were with you for so much of life's journey—for so much of the time it took—they helped you forget the changes that time wrought. The family is present no matter what experiences a person passes through, and no matter what rites mark that passage.

Whether birthdays are celebrated by peers or families, they are most important at the ages when each year is a remarkable achievement—at the beginning of life and the end of it. (212) Lucia's birthday was celebrated during the 1890s somewhere on the Eastern seaboard; besides this, we know no more than the delight on the face of the birthday child (behind the cake at right) tells us.

213

(213) *Linda's birthday was observed near New York City in the 1940s by her sister as well as mother and father, who provided a pile of presents and a cake but did not omit the milk intended to build strong bones. (214) The Maryland family who celebrated the eighty-fifth birthday of their grandmother in 1942 waited for her to blow out the candles that stand for years of life snuffed out.*

(215–17) *Infant baptism in the Christian church has traditionally represented a covenant between the parents and the religious community to bring up the child as a member of the faith. Whether in a modern living room, or in a Methodist church in San Antonio, Texas, or at a riverbank in the country-revivalist tradition, christening is a solemn rite, as the religious community pledges its willingness to augment the parents' instruction and serve, either with godparents or as a whole congregation, as a surrogate family.*

215

216

218

(218) *The Bar Mitzvah ceremony that admits a boy into the adult Jewish world at the age of thirteen emphasizes that he must now pull his weight in the community.* (219) *This Roman Catholic child's first communion entitles her in the future to direct participation in the service of the Mass. In both cases, a parent relinquishes some parental control to the religious community.*

220

(220) *Symbolizing the school in its role* in loco parentis, *the principal (with mustache) and only teacher (to his left) of the Parnassus, Pennsylvania, high school posed with their graduating class of 1902. The eleven students—there were only two boys because boys usually quit school after eighth grade and went to work—look like adults already and would be expected to assume adult roles with a minimum of time for fun. (221) In 1975 the graduation at Tufts University in Medford, Massachusetts, was recorded for these families by a photograph of two seniors with their grandmothers. In 1902 the percentage of students who went on to high school after the first compulsory eight grades was roughly the same as the percentage of students in 1975 who went on to college. It seems to take longer and longer, in some ways, to leave the family.*

Whether the family gathers to see the bride and groom off or the couple start their life together by themselves, a new family is in the making at every wedding and the mold of the old is broken. (222) The Nebraska couple who posed in wedding garb with their proud new parlor table in the 1880s stand like Adam and Eve, driven from the Garden of Eden and determined to build life anew on the Great Plains. (223) The aunts smirk while standing in a row behind the newlyweds at this Cooperstown, New York, wedding in 1915.

222

(224 a–f, 225) *A North Carolina tobacco-farm family married their daughter, Sherry, to a young neighbor and Vietnam veteran named Frankie in 1968. The wedding was unique and typical at the same time, as all basic rites are: For the participants it is all miraculous, but to the outsider it seems just like every other similar event. Sherry's father reacted with brusque grace to his unaccustomed tuxedo and the loss of a beloved daughter. (224 e) Doubtful about the tuxedo, he told a friend, "I usually wear what I have—today I wore more than I had." (224 d) Shaving, he remarked, "I am too tired to be dirty." And taking Sherry so proudly down the aisle, he must have remembered his answer to the minister's question at the rehearsal—"Who gives this woman . . . ?"—when he had replied, "I am going to lend her."*

A Golden Wedding anniversary in the 1890s and a Silver Wedding anniversary in 1972 both served as milestones for the principals. The family who clustered around the pair married fifty years that day proved the assertion of one etiquette book that a houseful of descendants was the best anniversary gift of all. The other couple was photographed next to an enlarged picture of themselves twenty-five years before: Clothing styles had changed, but, in the prime of life, they seemed to have grown better, not older.

226

227

228

229

The ultimate rite of passage is the funeral, marking a person's passage beyond family and the world. A procession like the one that took place at Bishop Potter's burial in Christ Episcopal churchyard in Cooperstown, New York, in 1908 (228) is an appropriately symbolic part of this rite. Victorian sentimentality about death was in part the defensive mechanism of an age when death was an omnipresent aspect of life. When cameras became generally available, they were sometimes used in a heart-wrenching attempt to slow the disappearance from memory of someone loved (229, 230). Both of these corpses were photographed in Albany, Minnesota, but thirty years apart; the baby was memorialized as he lay in his pine coffin, surrounded by flowers, in 1895. The man was photographed in 1925. Despite the introduction of the Ford to prairie farmers, trips to town were rare, and this may have been his only portrait. The older woman looks at the widow with concern, asserting the rights of the living over those of the dead.

231

(232) *At a soldier's funeral among his own mountain people in Kentucky in the 1940s, his mother gave way to a burst of grief that may have relieved her despair. The mourners, in their comforting gestures and solitary pain, resemble figures in a Greek frieze, bewailing the loss of the younger generation—the promise of the family—before the elder one.* (231) *A more tranquil funeral took place in Greene County, Georgia, in 1941, when a member of the prominent Boswell family was laid to rest. Kinsfolk in the cemetery seized the lull after the funeral to gossip and discuss genealogy and the tides of family affairs. There is no arena like the family for observing people in all conditions over the years.* (233) *A Mennonite hearse bears its lone burden to the graveyard in Blue Ball, Pennsylvania, in 1942.*

233

232

Couples: the source of family life—and the enduring family experience.

"Therefore shall a man leave his father and his mother, and shall cleave unto his wife; and they shall be one flesh."

Genesis, II, xxiv.

234

235

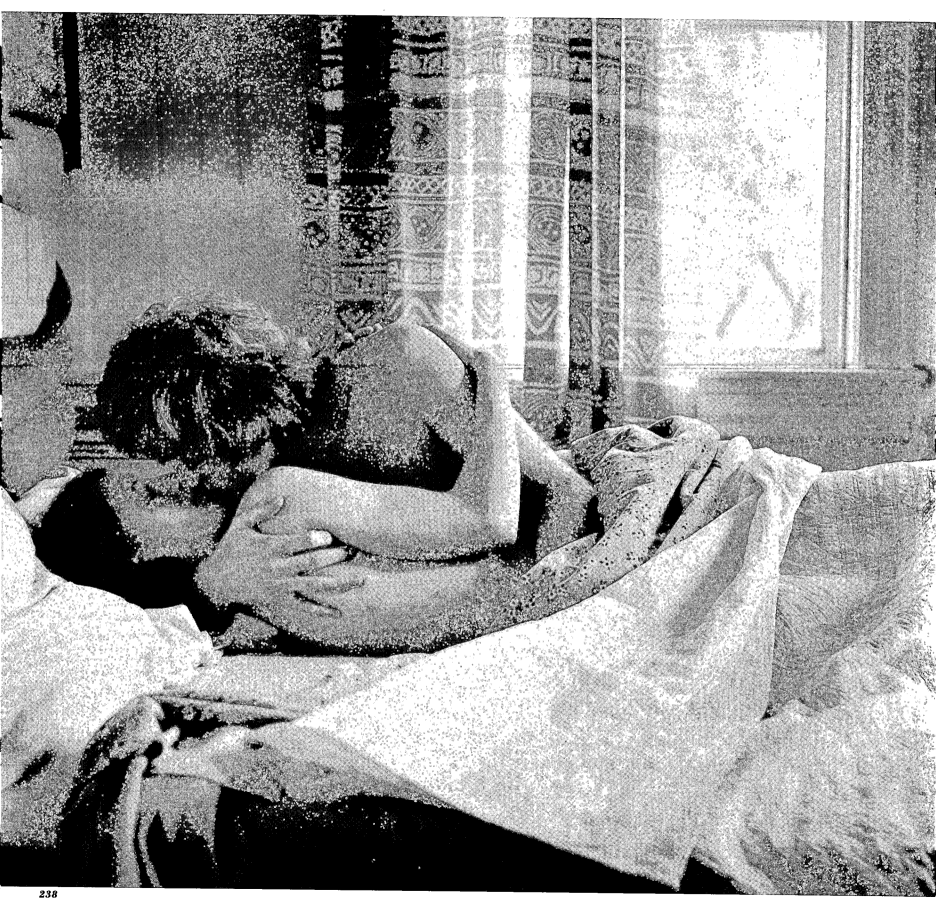